365 LOVE POEMS

365 LOVE POEMS

Compiled by John Gabriel Hunt

GRAMERCY BOOKS
New York • Avenel, New Jersey

Introduction
Copyright © 1993 by Outlet Book Company, Inc.
All rights reserved

This 1993 edition is published by Gramercy Books,
distributed by Outlet Book Company, Inc.,
a Random House Company,
40 Engelhard Avenue,
Avenel, New Jersey 07001.

Random House
New York • Toronto • London • Sydney • Auckland

Printed and bound in the United States

Library of Congress Cataloging-in-Publication Data
365 love poems / edited by John Gabriel Hunt.
p. cm.
ISBN 0-517-08684-0
1. Love poetry, English. 2. Love poetry, American.
I. Hunt, John Gabriel, 1952– .
II. Title: Three hundred sixty-five love poems.
PR1184.A15 1992
821.008′0354—dc20   92-31231   CIP

8 7 6 5 4 3 2 1

CONTENTS

INTRODUCTION

In a book of 365 love poems—one for every day of the year—the constant reappearance of certain phrases and sentiments might well be expected. But, perhaps surprisingly, each of these poems offers a fresh and personal view of love. Even lines that were written centuries ago speak of romantic concerns not unlike those of today, and the expression of those concerns remains amazingly vital and original. Sir Walter Raleigh, for example, gives this definition of love: "Now what is love; I pray thee, tell? / It is that fountain and that well / Where pleasure and repentance dwell." Robert Herrick lauds his lady's striking physical appearance: "When as in silks my Julia goes / Then, then (me thinks) how sweetly flows / The liquefaction of her clothes." John Donne laments the lack of time available to some lovers: "The poor, the foul, the false, love can / Admit, but not the busied man." And William Shakespeare praises a loved one with these immortal lines: "Shall I compare thee to a summer's day? / Thou art more lovely and more temperate."

Each poet, no matter when he or she lived, explores love in a new and revealing way. The emotions may be timeless and universal, but the language, imagery, ideas, and personal response within each love poem are invariably unique. These evocative poems range from the highly emotive declarations of Lord Byron ("She walks in beauty, like the night / Of cloudless climes and starry skies") and Elizabeth Barrett Browning ("I think of thee! My thoughts do twine and bud / About thee, as wild vines, about a tree") to the terse directness of Emily Dickinson ("Heart, we will forget him! / You and I, to-night!") and Carl Sandburg ("Your white shoulders / I remember / And your shrug of laughter").

Care has been taken to arrange the poems according to their themes, which should aid the reader who, on a particular day, may wish to dwell upon a paean to physical love rather than lost love, or vice versa. Some of the categories have an internal structure and subsections. "The Meaning of Love," for example, begins with poetry defining and praising love and ends with considerations of love-not-quite-so-wonderful. "The Anguish of Love" contains groups of poems reflecting absence, longing, suffering, and finally, anger and sarcasm. And "Declarations of Love" includes passionate odes addressed to and about loved ones, some of whom are named by the poets. But with a subject such as love, categories are artificial boundaries, and you will find that no matter in which section particular poems may appear, the sentiments expressed run the gamut of human emotions and encompass love in all its aspects.

JOHN GABRIEL HUNT

Avenel, New Jersey
1993

The

Meaning

of

Love

1 · NOW WHAT IS LOVE?

Now what is love, I pray thee, tell?
  It is that fountain and that well
  Where pleasure and repentance dwell;
  It is, perhaps, the saucing bell
  That tolls all into heaven or hell;
  And this is love, as I hear tell.

Yet what is love, I prithee, say?
  It is a work on holiday,
  It is December matched with May,
  When lusty bloods in fresh array
  Hear ten months after of the play;
  And this is love, as I hear say.

Yet what is love, good shepherd, sain?
  It is a sunshine mixed with rain,
  It is a toothache or like pain,
  It is a game where none hath gain;
  The lass saith no, yet would full fain;
  And this is love, as I hear sain.

Yet, shepherd, what is love, I pray?
  It is a yes, it is a nay,
  A pretty kind of sporting fray,
  It is a thing will soon away.
  Then, nymphs, take vantage while ye may;
  And this is love, as I hear say.

Yet what is love, good shepherd, show?
  A thing that creeps, it cannot go,
  A prize that passeth to and fro,
  A thing for one, a thing for moe,
  And he that proves shall find it so;
  And shepherd, this is love, I trow.

                         SIR WALTER RALEIGH

2 · LOVE AS THE THEME OF POETS

And said I that my limbs were old;
And said I that my blood was cold,
And that my kindly fire was fled,
And my poor withered heart was dead,
  And that I might not sing of love
How could I to the dearest theme,
That ever warmed a minstrel's dream,
  So foul, so false, a recreant prove!
How could I name love's very name,
Nor wake my harp to notes of flame!

In peace, Love tunes the shepherd's reed;
In war, he mounts the warrior's steed;
In halls, in gay attire is seen;
In hamlets, dances on the green.
Love rules the court, the camp, the grove,
And men below, and saints above;
For love is heaven, and heaven is love.

SIR WALTER SCOTT

3 · THE PRAISE OF LOVE

Fain would I change that note
  To which fond love hath charm'd me,
Long, long to sing by rote,
  Fancying that that harm'd me;
Yet when this thought doth come,
"Love is the perfect sum
  Of all delight,"
    I have no other choice
    Either for pen or voice
  To sing or write.

O Love, they wrong thee much
  That say thy sweet is bitter,
When thy rich fruit is such
  As nothing can be sweeter.
Fair house of joy and bliss
Where truest pleasure is,
  I do adore thee;
    I know thee what thou art,
    I serve thee with my heart,
  And fall before thee.

TOBIAS HUME

4 · SONNET

As an unperfect actor on the stage,
Who with his fear is put besides his part,
Or some fierce thing replete with too much rage,
Whose strength's abundance weakens his own heart;
So I, for fear of trust, forget to say
The perfect ceremony of love's rite.
And in mine own love's strength seem to decay,
O'ercharged with burthen of mine own love's might.
O, let my books be then the eloquence
And dumb presagers of my speaking breast;
Who plead for love, and look for recompense,
More than that tongue that more hath more express'd.
    O, learn to read what silent love hath writ:
    To hear with eyes belongs to love's fine writ.

WILLIAM SHAKESPEARE

5 · SONNET

Sweet Love, renew thy force; be it not said
Thy edge should blunter be than appetite,
Which but today by feeding is allay'd,
Tomorrow sharpen'd in his former might:
So, Love, be thou; although today thou fill
Thy hungry eyes even till they wink with fullness,
Tomorrow see again, and do not kill
The spirit of Love with a perpetual dullness.
Let this sad interim like the ocean be
Which parts the shore, where two contracted new
Come daily to the banks, that, when they see
Return of Love, more blest may be the view;
    Or call it winter, which, being full of care,
    Makes summer's welcome thrice more wish'd,
    more rare.

WILLIAM SHAKESPEARE

6 · SONNET

My love is strengthen'd, though more weak in seeming;
I love not less, though less the show appear;
That love is merchandized whose rich esteeming
The owner's tongue doth publish everywhere.
Our love was new, and then but in the spring,
When I was wont to greet it with my lays;
As Philomel in summer's front doth sing,
And stops her pipe in growth of riper days:
Not that the summer is less pleasant now
Than when her mournful hymns did hush the night,
But that wild music burthens every bough,
And sweets grown common lose their dear delight.
    Therefore, like her, I sometime hold my tongue,
    Because I would not dull you with my song.

WILLIAM SHAKESPEARE

7 · SONNET

Let me not to the marriage of true minds
Admit impediments. Love is not love
Which alters when it alteration finds,
Or bends with the remover to remove:
O, no! it is an ever-fixed mark,
That looks on tempests and is never shaken;
It is the star to every wandering bark,
Whose worth's unknown, although his height be taken.
Love's not Time's fool, though rosy lips and cheeks
Within his bending sickle's compass come;
Love alters not with his brief hours and weeks,
But bears it out even to the edge of doom.
    If this be error and upon me proved,
    I never writ, nor no man ever loved.

WILLIAM SHAKESPEARE

8 · ANSWER TO A CHILD'S QUESTION

Do you ask what the birds say? The sparrow, the dove,
The linnet, and thrush say, "I love, and I love!"
In the winter they're silent, the wind is so strong;
What it says I don't know, but it sings a loud song.
But green leaves, and blossoms, and sunny
    warm weather,
And singing and loving—all come back together.
But the lark is so brimful of gladness and love,
The green fields below him, the blue sky above,
That he sings, and he sings, and forever sings he,
"I love my love, and my love loves me."

SAMUEL TAYLOR COLERIDGE

9 · THE TORCH OF LOVE

The torch of love dispels the gloom
Of life, and animates the tomb;
But never let it idly flare
On gazers in the open air,
Nor turn it quite away from one
To whom it serves for moon and sun,
And who alike in night or day
Without it could not find his way.

WALTER SAVAGE LANDOR

10 · I WILL TELL THEE WHAT
IT IS TO LOVE

Love? I will tell thee what it is to love!
It is to build with human thoughts a shrine,
Where Hope sits brooding like a beauteous dove;
Where Time seems young, and Life a thing divine.
All tastes, all pleasures, all desires combine
To consecrate this sanctuary of bliss.
Above, the stars in cloudless beauty shine;
Around, the streams their flowery margins kiss;
And if there's heaven on earth, that heaven is surely this.

Yes, this is love, the steadfast and the true,
The immortal glory which hath never set;
The best, the brightest boon the heart e'er knew:
Of all life's sweets the very sweetest yet!
O' who but can recall the eve they met
To breathe, in some green walk, their first young vow?
While summer flowers with moonlight dews were wet,
And winds sighed soft around the mountain's brow,
And all was rapture then which is but memory now!

CHARLES SWAIN

11 · AH! WHAT IS LOVE?

Ah! what is love? It is a pretty thing,
As sweet unto a shepherd as a king,
    And sweeter too;
For kings have cares that wait upon a crown,
And cares can make the sweetest face to frown:
    Ah then, ah then,
If country loves such sweet desires gain,
What lady would not love a shepherd swain?

His flocks are folded; he comes home at night
As merry as a king in his delight,
    And merrier too;
For kings bethink them what the state require,
Where shepherds, careless, carol by the fire:
    Ah then, ah then,
If country love such sweet desires gain,
What lady would not love a shepherd swain?

He kisseth first, then sits as blithe to eat
His cream and curd as doth the king his meat,
    And blither too;
For kings have often fears when they sup,
Where shepherds dread no poison in their cup:
    Ah then, ah then,
If country loves such sweet desires gain,
What lady would not love a shepherd swain?

Upon his couch of straw he sleeps as sound
As doth the king upon his beds of down,
    More sounder too;
For cares cause kings full oft their sleep to spill,
Where weary shepherds lie and snort their fill:
    Ah then, ah then,
If country loves such sweet desires gain,
What lady would not love a shepherd swain?

Thus with his wife he spends the year as blithe
As doth the king at every tide or syth,
     And blither too;
For kings have wars and broils to take in hand,
When shepherds laugh, and love upon the land:
     Ah then, ah then,
If country loves such sweet desires gain,
What lady would not love a shepherd swain?

               ROBERT GREENE

12 · A LADY'S PRAYER
TO CUPID

Since I must needs into thy school return,
Be pitiful, O Love, and do not burn
Me with desire of cold and frozen age,
Nor let me follow a fond boy or page;
But, gentle Cupid, give me if you can
One to my love, whom I may call a man,
Of person comely, and of face as sweet;
Let him be sober, secret, and discreet,
Well practiced in Love's school; let him within
Wear all his beard, and none upon his chin.

               THOMAS CAREW

13 · UPON CUPID

Love, like a beggar, came to me
  With hose and doublet torn,
His shirt bedangling from his knee,
  With hat and shoes outworn.

He ask'd an alms; I gave him bread,
  And meat too, for his need;
Of which, when he had fully fed,
  He wished me all good speed.

Away he went; but as he turn'd,
  In faith I know not how,
He toucht me so, as that I burn,
  And am tormented now.

Love's silent flames, and fires obscure,
  Then crept into my heart;
And though I saw no bow, I'm sure
  His finger was the dart.

ROBERT HERRICK

14 · LOVE (1)

Immortal Love, author of this great frame,
  Sprung from that beauty which can never fade;
  How hath man parceled out thy glorious name,
And thrown it on that dust which thou hast made,
While mortal love doth all the title gain!
  Which siding with invention, they together
  Bear all the sway, possessing heart and brain,
(Thy workmanship) and give thee share in neither.
Wit fancies beauty, beauty raiseth wit:
  The world is theirs; they two play out the game,
  Thou standing by: and though thy glorious name
Wrought our deliverance from th' infernal pit,
  Who sings thy praise? Only a scarf or glove
  Doth warm our hands, and make them write of love.

GEORGE HERBERT

15 · LOVE (2)

Immortal Heat, O let thy greater flame
  Attract the lesser to it: let those fires,
  Which shall consume the world, first make it tame;
And kindle in our hearts such true desires,
As may consume our lusts, and make thee way.
  Then shall our hearts pant thee; then shall our brain
  All her invention on thine altar lay,
And there in hymns send back thy fire again:
Our eyes shall see thee, which before saw dust;
  Dust blown by wit, till that they both were blind:
  Thou shalt never recover all thy goods in kind,
Who wert diseased by usurping lust:
  All knees shall bow to thee; all wits shall rise,
  And praise him who did make and mend our eyes.

GEORGE HERBERT

The rising moon has hid the stars;
Her level rays, like golden bars,
  Lie on the landscape green,
  With shadows brown between.

And silver white the river gleams,
As if Diana, in her dreams,
  Had dropt her silver bow
  Upon the meadows low.

On such a tranquil night as this
She woke Endymion with a kiss,
  When, sleeping in the grove,
  He dreamed not of her love.

Like Dian's kiss, unasked, unsought,
Love gives itself, but is not bought;
  Nor voice, nor sound betrays
  Its deep, impassioned gaze.

It comes—the beautiful, the free,
The crown of all humanity—
  In silence and alone
  To seek the elected one.

It lifts the boughs, whose shadows deep
Are life's oblivion, the soul's sleep,
  And kisses the closed eyes
  Of him who slumbering lies.

O weary hearts! O slumbering eyes!
O drooping souls, whose destinies
  Are fraught with fear and pain,
  Ye shall be loved again!

No one is so accursed by fate,
No one so utterly desolate,
   But some heart, though unknown,
   Responds unto his own:

Responds—as if, with unseen wings,
An angel touched its quivering strings;
   And whispers, in its song,
   "Where hast thou stayed so long?"
                HENRY WADSWORTH LONGFELLOW

17 · LOVE

Yes, love indeed is light from heaven;
   A spark of that immortal fire
With angels shared, by Alla given,
   To lift from earth our low desire.
Devotion wafts the mind above,
But heaven itself descends in love;
A feeling from the Godhead caught,
To wean from self each sordid thought;
A ray of Him who formed the whole;
A glory circling round the soul!
                GEORGE GORDON, LORD BYRON

18 · BECAUSE I BREATHE NOT LOVE

Because I breathe not love to every one,
   Nor do not use set colors for to wear,
   Nor nourish special locks of vowed hair,
Nor give each speech a full point of a groan—
The courtly nymphs, acquainted with the moan
   Of them who on their lips Love's standard bear,
   "What! He?" say they of me. "Now I dare swear
He cannot love: No, no! let him alone."
   And think so still—if Stella know my mind.

Profess, indeed, I do not Cupid's art;
   But you, fair maids, at length this true shall find—
That his right badge is but worn in the heart.
   Dumb swans, not chattering pies, do lovers prove:
   They love indeed who quake to say they love.
SIR PHILIP SIDNEY

19 · LOVE WHAT IT IS

Love is a circle that doth restless move
In the same sweet eternity of love.
ROBERT HERRICK

20 · SONNET

All my thoughts always speak to me of love,
   Yet have between themselves such difference
   That while one bids me bow with mind and sense,
A second saith, "Go to: look thou above";
The third one, hoping, yields me joy enough;
   And with the last come tears, I scarce know whence:

All of them craving pity in sore suspense,
Trembling with fears that the heart knoweth of.
And thus, being all unsure which path to take,
    Wishing to speak I know not what to say,
    And lose myself in amorous wanderings:
Until (my peace with all of them to make),
    Unto mine enemy I needs must pray,
    My lady Pity, for the help she brings.

DANTE ALIGHIERI
translated by Dante Gabriel Rossetti

21 · SONNET

Love and the gentle heart are one same thing,
    Even as the wise man in his ditty saith.
    Each, of itself, would be such life in death
As rational soul bereft of reasoning.
'Tis Nature makes them when she loves: a king
    Love is, whose palace where he sojourneth
    Is call'd the Heart; there draws he quiet breath
At first, with brief or longer slumbering.
Then beauty seen in virtuous womankind
    Will make the eyes desire, and through the heart
    Send the desiring of the eyes again;
Where often it abides so long enshrined
    That Love at length out of his sleep will start.
    And women feel the same for worthy men.

DANTE ALIGHIERI
translated by Dante Gabriel Rossetti

22 · THE FAITHFUL
AND THE TRUE

Love lives beyond
The tomb, the earth, which fades like dew!
I love the fond,
The faithful, and the true.

Love lives in sleep,
The happiness of healthy dreams:
Eve's dews may weep,
But love delightful seems.

'Tis seen in flowers,
And in the morning's pearly dew;
In earth's green hours,
And in the heaven's eternal blue.

'Tis heard in spring
When light and sunbeams, warm and kind,
On angel's wing
Bring love and music to the mind.

And where is voice,
So young, so beautiful, and sweet
As nature's choice,
Where spring and lovers meet?

Love lives beyond
The tomb, the earth, the flowers, and dew.
I love the fond,
The faithful, young, and true.

JOHN CLARE

23 · SONNET

Yet, love, mere love, is beautiful indeed
And worthy of acceptation. Fire is bright,
Let temple burn, or flax. An equal light
Leaps in the flame from cedar-plank or weed.
And love is fire. And when I say at need
I love thee . . . mark! . . . *I love thee*—in thy sight
I stand transfigured, glorified aright,
With conscience of the new rays that proceed
Out of my face toward thine. There's nothing low
In love, when love the lowest: meanest creatures
Who love God, God accepts while loving so.
And what I *feel*, across the inferior features
Of what I *am*, doth flash itself, and show
How that great work of Love enhances Nature's.

ELIZABETH BARRETT BROWNING

24 · SONNET

If thou must love me, let it be for nought
Except for love's sake only. Do not say
"I love her for her smile . . . her look . . . her way
Of speaking gently . . . for a trick of thought
That falls in well with mine, and certes brought
A sense of pleasant ease on such a day"—
For these things in themselves beloved, may
Be changed, or change for thee—and love, so wrought
May be unwrought so. Neither love me for
Thine own dear pity's wiping my cheeks dry—
A creature might forget to weep, who bore
Thy comfort long, and lose thy love thereby!
But love me for love's sake, that evermore
Thou may'st love on, through love's eternity.

ELIZABETH BARRETT BROWNING

Smoothing soft the nestling head
Of a maiden fancy-led,
Thus a grave-eyed woman said:

"Richest gifts are those we make,
Dearer than the love we take
That we give for love's own sake.

"Well I know the heart's unrest;
Mine has been the common quest
To be loved and therefore blest.

"Favors undeserved were mine;
At my feet as on a shrine
Love has laid its gifts divine.

"Sweet the offerings seemed, and yet
With their sweetness came regret,
And a sense of unpaid debt.

"Heart of mine unsatisfied,
Was it vanity or pride
That a deeper joy denied?

"Hands that ope but to receive
Empty close; they only live
Richly who can richly give.

"Still," she sighed, with moistening eyes,
"Love is sweet in any guise;
But its best is sacrifice!

"He who, giving, does not crave
Likest is to Him who gave
Life itself the loved to save.

"Love, that self-forgetful gives,
Sows surprise of ripened sheaves,
Late or soon its own receives."
JOHN GREENLEAF WHITTIER

26 · LOVE

O power of Love, O wondrous mystery!
How is my dark illumined by thy light,
That maketh morning of my gloomy night,
Setting my soul from Sorrow's bondage free
With swift-sent revelation! Yea, I see
Beyond the limitation of my sight
And senses, comprehending now, aright,
Today's proportion to eternity.
Through thee, my faith in God is made more sure,
My searching eyes have pierced the misty veil;
The pain and anguish which stern Sorrow brings
Through thee become more easy to endure.
Love-strong I mount, and heaven's high summit scale;
Through thee, my soul has spread her folded wings.
KATRINA TRASK

All love that has not friendship for its base,
   Is like a mansion built upon the sand.
Though brave its walls as any in the land,
And its tall turrets lift their heads in grace;
Though skillful and accomplished artists trace
   Most beautiful designs on every hand,
   And gleaming statues in dim niches stand,
And fountains play in some flow'r-hidden place:

Yet, when from the frowning east a sudden gust
   Of adverse fate is blown, or sad rains fall
   Day in, day out, against its yielding wall,
Lo! the fair structure crumbles to the dust.
Love, to endure life's sorrow and earth's woe,
Needs friendship's solid masonwork below.

ELLA WHEELER WILCOX

28 · THEY SIN WHO TELL
LOVE CAN DIE

They sin who tell love can die,
With life all other passions fly,
All others are but vanity.
In heaven ambition cannot dwell,
Nor avarice in the vaults of hell:
Earthly these passions, as of earth,
They perish where they have their birth.
   But love is indestructible;
Its holy flame forever burneth,
From heaven it came, to heaven returneth.
Too oft on earth a troubled guest,
At times deceived, at times opprest;

It here is tried and purified,
And hath in heaven its perfect rest.
It soweth here with toil and care,
But the harvest-time of love is there.
Oh! when a mother meets on high
The babe she lost in infancy,
Hath she not then for pains and fears,
   The day of woe, the anxious night,
For all her sorrow, all her tears,
   An overpayment of delight?
ROBERT SOUTHEY

29 · MY DAY

O let the solid ground
   Not fail beneath my feet
Before my life has found
   What some have found so sweet;
Then let come what come may,
What matter if I go mad,
I shall have had my day.

Let the sweet heavens endure,
   Nor close and darken above me,
Before I am quite sure
   That there is one to love me;
Then let come what come may
To a life that has been so sad,
I shall have had my day.
ALFRED, LORD TENNYSON

30 · WHAT IS LOVE?

Now what is love I will thee tell:
It is the fountain and the well
Where pleasure and repentance dwell;
It is perhaps the sansing bell
That rings all in to heaven and hell,
And this is love, and this is love, as I hear tell.

Now what is love I will you show:
A thing that creeps and cannot go;
A prize that passeth to and fro;
A thing for me, a thing for mo':
And he that proves shall find it so,
And this is love, and this is love, sweet friend, I trow.

THOMAS HEYWOOD

31 · A WOMAN'S SHORTCOMINGS

Unless you can think, when the song is done,
  No other is soft in the rhythm;
Unless you can feel, when left by one,
  That all men else go with him;
Unless you can know, when unpraised by his breath,
  That your beauty itself wants proving;
Unless you can swear, "For life, for death!"—
  Oh fear to call it loving!

Unless you can muse in a crowd all day,
  On the absent face that fixed you;
Unless you love, as the angels may,
  With the breadth of heaven betwixt you;

Unless you can dream that his fast is fast,
  Through behoving and unbehoving;
Unless you can die when the dream is past—
  Oh never call it loving!
                    ELIZABETH BARRETT BROWNING

32 · LEAVE ME, O LOVE

Leave me, O Love, which reachest but to dust,
And thou my mind aspire to higher things:
Grow rich in that which never taketh rust:
Whatever fades, but fading pleasure brings.

Draw in thy beams, and humble all thy might,
To that sweet yoke, where lasting freedoms be:
Which breaks the clouds and opens forth the light,
That doth both shine and give us sight to see.

O take fast hold, let that light be thy guide,
In this small course which birth draws out to death,
And think how evil becometh him to slide,
Who seeketh heav'n, and comes of heav'nly breath.
  Then farewell, world, thy uttermost I see,
  Eternal Love, maintain thy life in me.
    Splendidis longum valedico nugis.
                    SIR PHILIP SIDNEY

33 · HE THAT LOVES
A ROSY CHEEK

He that loves a rosy cheek,
   Or a coral lip admires,
Or from starlike eyes doth seek
   Fuel to maintain his fires;
As old Time makes these decay,
So his flames must waste away.

But a smooth and steadfast mind,
   Gentle thoughts and calm desires,
Hearts with equal love combined,
   Kindle never-dying fires;
Where these are not, I despise
Lovely cheeks, or lips, or eyes.
               THOMAS CAREW

34 · ABSTINENCE

Abstinence sows sand all over
The ruddy limbs and flaming hair,
But Desire Gratified
Plants fruits of life and beauty there.
               WILLIAM BLAKE

35 · THE QUESTION ANSWERED

What is it men in women do require?
The lineaments of Gratified Desire.
What is it women do in men require?
The lineaments of Gratified Desire.

WILLIAM BLAKE

36 · I LAID ME DOWN
UPON A BANK

I laid me down upon a bank
Where Love lay sleeping.
I heard among the rushes dank
Weeping, weeping.

Then I went to the heath and the wild,
To the thistles and thorns of the waste,
And they told me how they were beguil'd,
Driven out, and compell'd to be chaste.

WILLIAM BLAKE

37 · NEVER GIVE ALL THE HEART

Never give all the heart, for love
Will hardly seem worth thinking of
To passionate women, if it seem
Certain, and they never dream
That it fades out from kiss to kiss;
For everything that's lovely is
But a brief dreamy kind delight.
O never give the heart outright
For they, for all smooth lips can say,
Have given their hearts up to the play.
And who could play it well enough
If deaf and dumb and blind with love?
He that made this knows all the cost
For he gave all his heart and lost.

WILLIAM BUTLER YEATS

38 · LOVE TO FAULTS
IS ALWAYS BLIND

Love to faults is always blind,
Always is to joy inclin'd,
Lawless, wing'd, and unconfin'd,
And breaks all chains from every mind.

Deceit to secrecy confin'd,
Lawful, cautious, and refin'd;
To everything but interest blind,
And forges fetters for the mind.

WILLIAM BLAKE

39 · A LECTURE UPON THE SHADOW

Stand still, and I will read to thee
A lecture, love, in love's philosophy.
    These three hours that we have spent,
    Walking here, two shadows went
Along with us, which we ourselves produced;
But, now the sun is just above our head,
    We do those shadows tread;
    And to brave clearness all things are reduced.
  So whilst our infant loves did grow,
  Disguises did, and shadows, flow,
  From us, and our care; but, now 'tis not so.

That love hath not attained the high'st degree,
Which is still diligent lest others see.

Except our loves at this noon stay,
We shall new shadows make the other way.
    As the first were made to blind
    Others; these which come behind
Will work upon ourselves, and blind our eyes.
If our loves faint, and westwardly decline;
    To me thou, falsely, thine,
    And I to thee mine actions shall disguise.
  The morning shadows wear away,
  But these grow longer all the day,
  But oh, love's day is short, if love decay.

Love is a growing, or full constant light;
And his first minute, after noon, is night.

JOHN DONNE

40 · MOST MEN KNOW LOVE

Most men know love but as a part of life;
They hide it in some corner of the breast,
Even from themselves; and only when they rest
In the brief pauses of that daily strife,
Wherewith the world might else be not so rife,
They draw it forth (as one draws forth a toy
To soothe some ardent, kiss-exacting boy)
And hold it up to sister, child, or wife.
Ah me! why may not love and life be one?
Why walk we thus alone, when by our side,
Love, like a visible God, might be our guide?
How would the marts grow noble! and the street,
Worn like a dungeon floor by weary feet,
Seem then a golden courtway of the sun!

HENRY TIMROD

41 · TO ELECTRA: LOVE
LOOKS FOR LOVE

Love, love begets; then never be
Unsoft to him who's smooth to thee:
Tigers and bears, I've heard some say,
For profer'd love, will love repay;
None are so harsh, but if they find
Softness in others, will be kind:
Affection will affection move,
Then you must like, because I love.

ROBERT HERRICK

42 · LOVE SEEKETH NOT ITSELF TO PLEASE

Love seeketh not itself to please,
   Nor for itself hath any care
But for another gives its ease,
   And builds a heaven in hell's despair.

Love seeketh only self to please,
   To bind another to its delight,
Joys in another's loss of ease,
   And builds a hell in heaven's despite.

WILLIAM BLAKE

43 · SONNET

With how sad steps, O Moon, thou climb'st the skies,
   How silently, and with how wan a face,
   What, may it be that even in heav'nly place
That busy archer his sharp arrows tries?
Sure if that long with love acquainted eyes
   Can judge of love, thou feel'st a lover's case;
   I read it in thy looks, thy languish'd grace,
To me that feel the like, thy state descries.
   Then ev'n of fellowship, O Moon, tell me
Is constant love deem'd there but want of wit?
Are beauties there as proud as here they be?
Do they above love to be lov'd, and yet
   Those lovers scorn whom that love doth possess?
   Do they call virtue there ungratefulness?

SIR PHILIP SIDNEY

44 · LOVE'S LIGHT IS STRANGE TO YOU?

Love's light is strange to you? Ah, me!
   Your heart is an unquickened seed,
And whatsoe'er your fortunes be,
   I tell you, you are poor indeed.

What toucheth it, it maketh bright,
   Yet loseth nothing, like the sun,
Within whose great and gracious light
   A thousand dewdrops shine as one.

ALICE CARY

45 · MODERN LOVE

And what is love? It is a doll dress'd up
For idleness to cosset, nurse, and dandle;
A thing of soft misnomers, so divine
That silly youth doth think to make itself
Divine by loving, and so goes on
Yawning and doting a whole summer long,
Till miss's comb is made a pearl tiara,
And common Wellingtons turn Romeo boots;
Then Cleopatra lives at number seven,
And Antony resides in Brunswick Square.
Fools! if some passions high have warm'd the world,
If queens and soldiers have play'd deep for hearts,
It is no reason why such agonies
Should be more common than the growth of weeds.
Fools! make me whole again that weighty pearl
The queen of Egypt melted, and I'll say
That ye may love in spite of beaver hats.

JOHN KEATS

46 · LOVE IS A SICKNESS

Love is a sickness full of woes,
    All remedies refusing;
A plant that most with cutting grows,
    Most barren with best using.
            Why so?
More we enjoy it, more it dies;
If not enjoyed, it sighing cries
            Heigh-ho!

Love is a torment of the mind,
    A tempest everlasting;
And Jove hath made it of a kind,
    Not well, nor full, nor fasting.
            Why so?
More we enjoy it, more it dies;
If not enjoyed, it' sighing cries,
            Heigh-ho!

SAMUEL DANIEL

47 · WE OUTGROW LOVE

We outgrow love like other things
    And put it in the drawer,
Till it an antique fashion shows
    Like costumes grandsires wore.

EMILY DICKINSON

48 · SWEET PERIL

Alas, how easily things go wrong!
A sigh too much, or a kiss too long,
And there follows a mist and a weeping rain,
And life is never the same again.

Alas, how hardly things go right!
'Tis hard to watch in a summer night,
For the sigh will come, and the kiss will stay,
And the summer night is a wintry day.

And yet how easily things go right,
If the sigh and a kiss of a summer's night
Come deep from the soul in the stronger ray
That is born in the light of the winter's day.

And things can never go badly wrong
If the heart be true and the love be strong,
For the mist, if it comes, and the weeping rain
Will be changed by the love into sunshine again.

GEORGE MACDONALD

Young

Love

49 · FIRST LOVE

I ne'er was struck before that hour
  With love so sudden and so sweet;
Her face it bloomed like a sweet flower
  And stole my heart away complete.
My face turned pale a deadly pale,
  My legs refused to walk away,
And when she looked what could I ail
My life and all seemed turned to clay.

And then my blood rushed to my face
  And took my eyesight quite away;
The trees and bushes round the place
  Seemed midnight at noon day.
I could not see a single thing,
  Words from my eyes did start;
They spoke as chords do from the string
  And blood burnt round my heart.

Are flowers the winter's choice?
  Is love's bed always snow?
She seemed to hear my silent voice
  Not love's appeals to know.
I never saw so sweet a face
  As that I stood before;
My heart has left its dwelling place
  And can return no more.

JOHN CLARE

50 · ON CELIA SINGING

You that think love can convey
    No other way
But through the eyes into the heart
    His fatal dart;
Close up their casements, and but hear
    This syren sing,
    And on the wing
Of her sweet voice it shall appear
That love can enter at the ear.

Then unveil your eyes, behold
    The curious mold
Where that voice dwells; and as we know
    When the cocks crow
    We freely may
    Gaze on the day,
So may you, when the music's done,
Awake and see the rising sun.

                 THOMAS CAREW

51 · THE YOUNG MAN'S SONG

I whispered, "I am too young,"
And then, "I am old enough";
Wherefore I threw a penny
To find out if I might love;
"Go and love, go and love, young man,
If the lady be young and fair."
Ah, penny, brown penny, brown penny,
I am looped in the loops of her hair.

Oh love is the crooked thing,
There is nobody wise enough
To find out all that is in it,
For he would be thinking of love
Till the stars had run away,
And the shadows eaten the moon;
Ah, penny, brown penny, brown penny.
One cannot begin it too soon.

WILLIAM BUTLER YEATS

52 · TO VIRGINS,
TO MAKE MUCH OF TIME

Gather ye rosebuds while ye may,
    Old Time is still a-flying:
And this same flower that smiles today,
    Tomorrow will be dying.

The glorious lamp of heaven, the Sun,
    The higher he's a-getting
The sooner will his race be run,
    And nearer he's to setting.

That age is best which is the first,
    When youth and blood are warmer;
But being spent, the worse, and worst
    Times, still succeed the former.

Then be not coy, but use your time;
    And while ye may, go marry:
For having lost but once your prime,
    You may for ever tarry.

ROBERT HERRICK

"Yes," I answered you last night;
  "No," this morning, sir, I say.
Colors seen by candlelight
  Will not look the same by day.

When the viols played their best,
  Lamps above, and laughs below,
Love me sounded like a jest,
  Fit for *yes* or fit for *no*.

Call me false or call me free,
  Vow, whatever light may shine,
No man on your face shall see
  Any grief for change on mine.

Yet the sin is on us both;
  Time to dance is not to woo;
Wooing light makes fickle troth.
  Scorn of *me* recoils on *you*.

Learn to win a lady's faith
  Nobly, as the thing is high,
Bravely, as for life and death,
  With a loyal gravity.

Lead her from the festive boards,
  Point her to the starry skies,
Guard her, by your truthful words,
  Pure from courtship's flatteries.

By your truth she shall be true,
  Ever true, as wives of yore;
And her *yes*, once said to you,
  Shall be Yes forevermore.
      ELIZABETH BARRETT BROWNING

54 · SONNET

I felt a spirit of love begin to stir
  Within my heart, long time unfelt till then;
  And saw Love coming towards me fair and fain
(That I scarce knew him for his joyful cheer),
Saying, "Be now indeed my worshipper!"
  And in his speech he laughed and laughed again.
  Then, while it was his pleasure to remain,
I chanced to look the way he had drawn near,
And saw the Ladies Joan and Beatrice
  Approach me, this the other following,
One and a second marvel instantly.
And even as now my memory speaketh this,
Love spake it then: "The first is christened Spring;
  The second Love, she is so like to me."

DANTE ALIGHIERI
translated by Dante Gabriel Rossetti

55 · THE EXCHANGE

We pledged our hearts, my love and I,
  I in my arms the maiden clasping;
I could not tell the reason why,
  But, O, I trembled like an aspen!

Her father's love she bade me gain;
  I went, and shook like any reed!
I strove to act the man—in vain!
  We had exchanged our hearts indeed.

SAMUEL TAYLOR COLERIDGE

Ah, how sweet it is to love!
  Ah, how gay is young desire!
And what pleasing pains we prove
  When we first approach love's fire!
Pains of love are sweeter far
Than all other pleasures are.

Sighs which are from lovers blown
  Do but gently heave the heart:
E'en the tears they shed alone
  Cure, like trickling balm, their smart.
Lovers, when they lose their breath,
Bleed away in easy death.

Love and Time with reverence use,
  Treat them like a parting friend:
Nor the golden gifts refuse
  Which in youth sincere they send:
For each year their price is more,
And they less simple than before.

Love, like spring-tides full and high,
  Swells in every youthful vein:
But each tide does less supply,
  Till they quite shrink in again.
If a flow in age appear,
'Tis but rain, and runs not clear.

JOHN DRYDEN

It was not in the winter
  Our loving lot was cast;
It was the Time of Roses—
  We pluck'd them as we pass'd!

'Twas twilight, and I bade you go,
  But still you held me fast;
It was the Time of Roses—
  We pluck'd them as we pass'd!

What else could peer thy glowing cheek,
  That tears began to stud?
And when I ask'd the like of Love,
  You snatch'd a damask bud,

And oped it to the dainty core,
  Still glowing to the last;
It was the Time of Roses—
  We pluck'd them as we pass'd!

THOMAS HOOD

O Mary, at thy window be!
   It is the wished, the trysted hour!
Those smiles and glances let me see
   That make the miser's treasure poor:
How blithely wad I bide the stoure,
   A weary slave frae sun to sun,
Could I the rich reward secure,
   The lovely Mary Morison.

Yestreen when to the trembling string
   The dance gaed through the lighted ha',
To thee my fancy took its wing—
   I sat, but neither heard nor saw:
Though this was fair, and that was braw,
   And yon the toast of a' the town,
I sighed, and said amang them a',
   "Ye are na Mary Morison."

O Mary, canst thou wreck his peace,
   Wha for thy sake wad gladly dee
Or canst thou break that heart of his,
   Whase only faut is loving thee?
If love for love thou wilt na gie,
   At least be pity to me shown;
A thought ungentle canna be
   The thought o' Mary Morison.

ROBERT BURNS

59 · FREEDOM AND LOVE

How delicious is the winning
Of a kiss at love's beginning,
When two mutual hearts are sighing
For the knot there's no untying!

Yet remember, 'midst our wooing,
Love has bliss, but Love has ruing;
Other smiles may make you fickle,
Tears for other charms may trickle.

Love he comes, and Love he tarries,
Just as fate or fancy carries;
Longest stays, when sorest chidden;
Laughs and flies, when press'd and bidden.

Bind the sea to slumber stilly,
Bind its odor to the lily,
Bind the aspen ne'er to quiver,
Then bind Love to last forever.

Love's a fire that needs renewal
Of fresh beauty for its fuel:
Love's wing moults when caged and captured,
Only free, he soars enraptured.

Can you keep the bee from ranging
Or the ringdove's neck from changing?
No! nor fetter'd Love from dying
In the knot there's no untying.

THOMAS CAMPBELL

Often when the night is come,
With its quiet group at home,
While they broider, knit, or sew,
Read, or chat in voices low,
Suddenly you lift your eyes
With an earnest look, and wise;
But I cannot read their lore,
Tell me less, or tell me more.

Like a picture in a book,
Pure and peaceful is your look,
Quietly you walk your ways;
Steadfast duty fills the days.
Neither tears nor fierce delights,
Feverish days nor tossing nights,
Any troublous dreams confess—
Tell me more, or tell me less.

Swift the weeks are on the wing;
Years are brief, and love a thing
Blooming, fading, like a flower;
Wake and seize the little hour.
Give me welcome, or farewell;
Quick! I wait! And who can tell
What tomorrow may befall—
Love me more, or not at all.

EDWARD ROWLAND SILL

61 · FIRST LOVE

Ah! I remember well (and how can I
But evermore remember well?) when first
Our flame began, when scarce we knew what was
The flame we felt; when as we sat and sighed
And looked upon each other, and conceived
Not what we ail'd—yet something we did ail;
And yet were well, and yet we were not well,
And what was our disease we could not tell.
Then would we kiss, then sigh, then look; and thus
In that first garden of our simpleness
We spent our childhood. But when years began
To reap the fruit of knowledge, ah, how then
Would she with graver looks, with sweet stern brow
Check my presumption and my forwardness?
Yet still would give me flowers, still would me show
What she would have me, yet not have me know.

SAMUEL DANIEL

Young Love lies sleeping
   In Maytime of the year,
Among the lilies,
   Lapped in the tender light:
White lambs come grazing,
   White doves come building there:
And round about him
   The May-bushes are white.

Soft moss the pillow
   For oh, a softer cheek;
Broad leaves cast shadow
   Upon the heavy eyes:
There winds and waters
   Grow lulled and scarcely speak;
There twilight lingers
   The longest in the skies.

Young Love lies dreaming;
   But who shall tell the dream?
A perfect sunlight
   On rustling forest tips;
Or perfect moonlight
   Upon a rippling stream;
Or perfect silence,
   Or song of cherished lips.

Burn odors round him
   To fill the drowsy air;
Weave silent dances
   Around him to and fro;
For oh, in waking
   The sights are not so fair,
And song and silence
   Are not like these below.

Young Love lies dreaming
    Till summer days are gone—
Dreaming and drowsing
    Away to perfect sleep:
He sees the beauty
    Sun hath not looked upon,
And tastes the fountain
    Unutterably deep.

Him perfect music
    Doth hush unto his rest,
And through the pauses
    The perfect silence calms:
Oh, poor the voices
    Of earth from east to west,
And poor earth's stillness
    Between her stately palms!

Young Love lies drowsing
    Away to poppied death;
Cool shadows deepen
    Across the sleeping face:
So fails the summer
    With warm delicious breath
And what hath autumn
    To give us in its place?

Draw close the curtain
    Of branchèd evergreen;
Change cannot touch them
    With fading fingers sere:
Here the first violets
    Perhaps will bud unseen,
And a dove, maybe,
    Return to nestle here.
                    CHRISTINA ROSSETTI

63 · AN ANECDOTE OF LOVE

When April and dew brings primroses here
I think love of you at the spring o' the year.
Did I harbor bad words when your garter fell off?
I to stoop was deterred but I stood not to scoff.
A bit of brown list of small value must be,
But as it lay there 'twas a diamond to me.

Ere back you turned to pick it up
I noticed well the place,
For children there for violets stoop
With many a rosy face.
I fain would stoop myself you see
But dare not well presume;
The blackbird sung out let it be,
The maid was in her bloom.

How beautiful that ankle was
From which that garter fell,
And lusty was the bonny lass
Whose name I dare not tell.
I know the color of her gown
Her bonnet ribbon too;
The fairest maiden in the town
Is she that wears the blue.

Though years have gone but when I see
The green spot where it fell,
The stitchwort flower delighteth me
There blooming in the dell.
And years may come no winter seers
The green haunts of the dove,
Those wild flowers stand the blight of years
Sweet anecdotes of love.

JOHN CLARE

64 · THE GOOD MORROW

I wonder by my troth, what thou and I
   Did, till we loved? Were we not weaned till then?
But sucked on country pleasures, childishly?
   Or snorted we i'the seven sleepers' den?
'Twas so; but this, all pleasures fancies be.
   If ever any beauty I did see,
Which I desired, and got, 'twas but a dream of thee.

And now good morrow to our waking souls,
   Which watch not one another out of fear;
For love, all love of other sights controls,
   And makes one little room, an everywhere.
   Let sea-discoverers to new worlds have gone,
   Let maps to others, worlds on worlds have shown,
Let us possess our world, each hath one, and is one.

My face in thine eye, thine in mine appears,
   And true plain hearts do in the faces rest,
Where can we find two better hemispheres
   Without sharp North, without declining West?
   Whatever dies, was not mixed equally;
   If our two loves be one, or, thou and I
Love so alike, that none do slacken, none can die.

JOHN DONNE

Fly not yet—'tis just the hour
When pleasure, like the midnight flower,
That scorns the eye of vulgar light,
Begins to bloom for sons of night,
    And maids who love the moon!
'Twas but to bless these hours of shade
That beauty and the moon were made;
'Tis then their soft attractions glowing
Set the tides and goblets flowing!
    O! stay—O! stay—
Joy so seldom weaves a chain
Like this tonight, that O! 'tis pain
    To break its links so soon.

Fly not yet! the fount that played,
In times of old, through Ammon's shade,
Though icy cold by day it ran,
Yet still, like sounds of mirth, began
    To burn when night was near;
And thus should woman's heart and looks
At noon be cold as winter brooks,
Nor kindle till the night, returning,
Brings their genial hour for burning.
    O! stay—O! stay—
When did morning ever break
And find such beaming eyes awake
    As those that sparkle here!

THOMAS MOORE

66 · A BIRTHDAY

My heart is like a singing bird
   Whose nest is in a watered shoot;
My heart is like an apple tree
   Whose boughs are bent with thickset fruit:
My heart is like a rainbow shell
   That paddles in a halcyon sea;
My heart is gladder than all these
   Because my love is come to me.

Raise me a dais of silk and down;
   Hang it with vair and purple dyes;
Carve it in doves, and pomegranates,
   And peacocks with a hundred eyes;
Work it in gold and silver grapes,
   In leaves, and silver fleur-de-lys;
Because the birthday of my life
   Is come, my love is come to me.

CHRISTINA ROSSETTI

67 · THE LOVE KNOT

Tying her bonnet under her chin,
She tied her raven ringlets in;
But not alone in the silken snare
Did she catch her lovely floating hair,
For, tying her bonnet under her chin,
She tied a young man's heart within.

They were strolling together up the hill,
Where the wind comes blowing merry and chill;
And it blew the curls, a frolicsome race,
All over the happy peach-colored face,
Till, scolding and laughing, she tied them in,
Under her beautiful dimpled chin.

And it blew a color, bright as the bloom
Of the pinkest fuchsia's tossing plume,
All over the cheeks of the prettiest girl
That ever imprisoned a romping curl,
Or, tying her bonnet under her chin,
Tied a young man's heart within.

Steeper and steeper grew the hill;
Madder, merrier, chillier still
The western wind blew down, and played
The wildest tricks with the little maid,
As, tying her bonnet under her chin,
She tied a young man's heart within.

O western wind, do you think it was fair
To play such tricks with her floating hair?
To gladly, gleefully do your best
To blow her against the young man's breast,
Where he as gladly folded her in,
And kissed her mouth and her dimpled chin?

Ah! Ellery Vane, you little thought,
An hour ago, when you besought
This country lass to walk with you,
After the sun had dried the dew,
What perilous danger you'd be in,
As she tied her bonnet under her chin!

NORA PERRY

68 · SONNET

O beauty, passing beauty! Sweetest sweet!
  How canst thou let me waste my youth in sighs?
I only ask to sit beside thy feet.
  Thou knowest I dare not look into thine eyes.
Might I but kiss thy hand! I dare not fold
  My arms about thee—scarcely dare to speak.
And nothing seems to me so wild and bold,
  As with one kiss to touch thy blessed cheek.
Methinks if I should kiss thee, no control
  Within the thrilling brain could keep afloat,
  The subtle spirit. Even while I spoke,
The bare word *kiss* hath made my inner soul
  To tremble like a lustering, ere the note
  Hath melted in the silence that it broke.

ALFRED, LORD TENNYSON

Still sits the schoolhouse by the road,
  A ragged beggar sunning;
Around it still the sumachs grow,
  And blackberry vines are running.

Within, the master's desk is seen,
  Deep scarred by raps official;
The warping floor, the battered seats,
  The jackknife's carved initial;

The charcoal frescoes on its wall;
  Its door's worn sill, betraying
The feet that, creeping slow to school,
  Went storming out to playing!

Long years ago a winter sun
  Shone over it at setting;
Lit up its western windowpanes,
  And low eaves' icy fretting.

It touched the tangled golden curls,
  And brown eyes full of grieving,
Of one who still her steps delay
  When all the school were leaving.

For near her stood the little boy
  Her childish favor singled;
His cap pulled low upon a face
  Where pride and shame were mingled.

Pushing with restless feet the snow
  To right and left, he lingered;
As restlessly her tiny hands
  The blue-checked apron fingered.

He saw her lift her eyes; he felt
    The soft hand's light caressing,
And heard the tremble of her voice,
    As if a fault confessing.

"I'm sorry that I spelt the word:
    I hate to go above you,
Because"—the brown eyes lower fell—
    "Because, you see, I love you!"

Still memory to a gray-haired man
    That sweet child-face is showing.
Dear girl! The grasses on her grave
    Have forty years been growing!

He lives to learn, in life's hard school,
    How few who pass above him
Lament their triumph and his loss,
    Like her—because they love him.
                JOHN GREENLEAF WHITTIER

70 · KISSES

My love and I for kisses played:
    She would keep stakes—I was content;
But when I won, she would be paid;
    This made me ask her what she meant.
"Pray, since I see," quoth she, "your wrangling vein,
    Take your own kisses; give me mine again."
                WILLIAM STRODE

71 · SONNET

I wish I could remember that first day,
  First hour, first moment of your meeting me,
  If bright or dim the season, it might be
Summer or winter for aught I can say;
So unrecorded did it slip away,
  So blind was I to see and to foresee,
  So dull to mark the budding of my tree
That would not blossom yet for many a May.
If only I could recollect it, such
  A day of days! I let it come and go
  As traceless as a thaw of bygone snow;
It seemed to mean so little, meant so much;
If only now I could recall that touch,
  First touch of hand in hand—did one but know!

                      CHRISTINA ROSSETTI

72 · SONNET

First time he kissed me, he but only kissed
The fingers of this hand wherewith I write;
And ever since, it grew more clean and white . . .
Slow to world-greetings, quick with its "Oh, list,"
When the angels speak. A ring of amethyst
I could not wear here, plainer to my sight,
Than that first kiss. The second passed in height
The first, and sought the forehead, and half missed,
Half falling on the hair. O beyond meed!
That was the chrism of love, which love's own crown
With sanctifying sweetness, did precede.
The third upon my lips was folded down
In perfect, purple state; since when, indeed,
I have been proud and said, "My love, my own."

              ELIZABETH BARRETT BROWNING

Declarations

of

Love

The dawning of morn, the daylight's sinking,
The night's long hours still find me thinking
    Of thee, thee, only thee.
When friends are met, and goblets crown'd,
  And smiles are near that once enchanted,
Unreach'd by all that sunshine round,
    My soul, like some dark spot, is haunted
    By thee, thee, only thee.

Whatever in fame's high path could waken
My spirit once is now forsaken
    For thee, thee, only thee.
Like shores by which some headlong bark
  To the ocean hurries, resting never,
Life's scenes go by me, bright or dark
    I know not, heed not, hastening ever
    To thee, thee, only thee.

I have not a joy but of thy bringing,
And pain itself seems sweet when springing
    From thee, thee, only thee.
Like spells that nought on earth can break,
  Till lips that know the charm have spoken,
This heart, howe'er the world may wake
    Its grief, its scorn, can but be broken
    By thee, thee, only thee.

THOMAS MOORE

74 · MY LUVE IS LIKE
A RED, RED ROSE

O, my luve's like a red, red rose,
    That's newly sprung in June;
O, my luve's like the melodie
    That's sweetly play'd in tune.

As fair art thou, my bonnie lass,
    So deep in luve am I;
And I will luve thee still, my dear,
    Till a' the seas gang dry.

Till a' the seas gang dry, my dear,
    And the rocks melt wi' the sun;
I will luve thee still, my dear,
    While the sands of life shall run.

And fare thee weel, my only luve!
    And fare thee weel a while!
And I will come again, my luve,
    Tho' it were ten thousand mile.
                      ROBERT BURNS

75 · LOVE'S INFINITENESS

If yet I have not all thy love,
    Dear, I shall never have it all,
I cannot breathe one other sigh, to move,
    Nor can entreat one other tear to fall.
And all my treasure, which should purchase thee,
    Sighs, tears, and oaths, and letters I have spent,
Yet no more can be due to me
    Than at the bargain made was meant:

If then thy gift of love were partial,
That some to me, some should to others fall,
Dear, I shall never have thee all.

Or if then thou gavest me all,
   All was but all, which thou hadst then;
But if in thy heart, since, there be or shall
   New love created be, by other men,
Which have their stocks entire, and can in tears,
   In sighs, in oaths, and letters outbid me,
This new love may beget new fears,
   For this love was not vowed by thee.
And yet it was, thy gift being general,
The ground, thy heart is mine, whatever shall
Grow there, dear, I should have it all.

Yet I would not have all yet;
   He that hath all can have no more;
And since my love doth every day admit
   New growth, thou shouldst have new rewards in
      store:
Thou canst not every day give me thy heart;
   If thou canst give it, then thou never gavest it.

Love's riddles are that though thy heart depart
   It stays at home, and thou, with losing, savest it:
But we will have a way more liberal
Than changing hearts—to join them; so we shall
Be one, and one another's all.

                                   JOHN DONNE

So well I love thee, as without thee I
Love nothing; if I might choose, I'd rather die
Than be one day debarr'd thy company.

Since beasts, and plants do grow, and live and move,
Beasts are those men, that such a life approve:
He only lives, that deadly is in love.

The corn that in the ground is sown first dies
And of one seed do many ears arise:
Love, this world's corn, by dying multiplies.

The seeds of love first by thy eyes were thrown
Into a ground untill'd, a heart unknown
To bear such fruit, till by thy hands 'twas sown.

Look as your looking-glass by chance may fall,
Divide and break in many pieces small
And yet shows forth the selfsame face in all:

Proportions, features, graces just the same,
And in the smallest piece as well the name
Of fairest one deserves, as in the richest frame.

So all my thoughts are pieces but of you
Which put together makes a glass so true
As I therein no other's face but yours can view.

MICHAEL DRAYTON

77 · SONNET

Bright star! would I were steadfast as thou art—
   Not in lone splendor hung aloft the night
And watching, with eternal lids apart,
   Like nature's patient, sleepless Eremite,
The moving waters at their priestlike task
   Of pure ablution round earth's human shores,
Or gazing on the new soft fallen mask
   Of snow upon the mountains and the moors—
No—yet still steadfast, still unchangeable,
   Pillow'd upon my fair love's ripening breast,
To feel forever its soft fall and swell,
   Awake forever in a sweet unrest,
Still, still to hear her tender-taken breath,
And so live ever—or else swoon to death.

JOHN KEATS

78 · SONNET

Your hands lie open in the long fresh grass,
The finger-points look through like rosy blooms;
Your eyes smile peace. The pasture gleams and glooms
'Neath billowing skies that scatter and amass.
All round our nest, far as the eye can pass,
Are golden kingcup-fields with silver edge
Where the cow-parsley skirts the hawthorn-hedge.
'Tis visible silence, still as the hourglass.
Deep in the sun-searched growths the dragonfly
Hangs like a blue thread loosened from the sky.
So this winged hour is dropt to us from above.
Oh! clasp we to our hearts, for deathless dower,
This close-companioned inarticulate hour
When twofold silence was the song of love.

DANTE GABRIEL ROSSETTI

I fill this cup to one made up
  Of loveliness alone,
A woman, of her gentle sex
  The seeming paragon;
To whom the better elements
  And kindly stars have given
A form so fair, that, like the air,
  'Tis less of earth than heaven.

Her every tone is music's own,
  Like those of morning birds,
And something more than melody
  Dwells ever in her words;
The coinage of her heart are they,
  And from her lips each flows
As one may see the burdened bee
  Forth issue from the rose.

Affections are as thoughts to her,
  The measures of her hours;
Her feelings have the fragrancy,
  The freshness of young flowers;
And lovely passions, changing oft,
  So fill her, she appears
The image of themselves by turns—
  The idol of past years!

Of her bright face one glance will trace
  A picture on the brain,
And of her voice in echoing hearts
  A sound must long remain;
But memory, such as mine of her,
  So very much endears,
When death is nigh my latest sigh
  Will not be life's, but hers.

I fill this cup to one made up
  Of loveliness alone,
A woman, of her gentle sex
  The seeming paragon—
Her health! and would on earth there stood
  Some more of such a frame,
That life might be all poetry,
  And weariness a name.

EDWARD COATE PINKNEY

80 · HOW MANY TIMES?

How many times do I love thee, dear?
  Tell me how many thoughts there be
      In the atmosphere
      Of a new-fallen year,
Whose white and sable hours appear
  The latest flake of eternity:
So many things do I love thee, dear.

How many times do I love, again?
  Tell me how many beads there are
      In a silver chain
      Of the evening rain,
Unraveled from the tumbling main,
  And threading the eye of a yellow star:
So many times do I love, again.

THOMAS LOVELL BEDDOES

81 · SONNET

One day I wrote her name upon the strand,
But came the waves and washed it away:
Again I wrote it with a second hand,
But came the tide, and made my pains his prey.
Vain man, said she, that dost in vain assay
A mortal thing so to immortalize,
For I myself shall like to this decay,
And eke my name be wiped out likewise.
Not so (quod I), let baser things devise
To die in dust, but you shall live by fame:
My verse your virtues rare shall eternize,
And in the heavens write your glorious name:
Where, whenas Death shall all the world subdue,
Our love shall live, and later life renew.

EDMUND SPENSER

82 · THERE IS NONE,
O NONE BUT YOU

There is none, O none but you,
   That from me estrange the sight,
Whom mine eyes affect to view,
   And chained ears hear with delight.

Other beauties others move:
   In you I all graces find;
Such is the effect of love,
   To make them happy that are kind.

Women in frail beauty trust,
   Only seem you fair to me:

Still prove truly kind and just,
  For that may not dissembled be.

Sweet, afford me then your sight,
  That, surveying all your looks,
Endless volumes I may write,
  And fill the world with envied books:

Which, when after-ages view,
  All shall wonder and despair—
Woman, to find a man so true,
  Or man, a woman half so fair!

                    THOMAS CAMPION

83 · THE BURDEN OF LOVE

I bear an unseen burden constantly;
Waking or sleeping I can never thrust
The load aside; through summer's heat and dust
And winter's snows it still abides with me.
I cannot let it fall, though I should be
Never so weary; carry it I must.
Nor can the bands that bind it on me rust
Or break, nor ever shall I be set free.
Sometimes 'tis heavy as the weight that bore
Atlas on giant shoulders; sometimes light
As the frail message of the carrier dove;
But, light or heavy, shifting nevermore.
What is it thus oppressing, day and night?
The burden, dearest, of a mighty love.

                    LUCY WHITE JENNISON

Shall I love you like the wind, love,
  That is so fierce and strong,
That sweeps all barriers from its path
  And reeks not right or wrong?
The passion of the wind, love,
  Can never last for long.

Shall I love you like the fire, love,
  With furious heat and noise,
To waken in you all love's fears
  And little of love's joys?
The passion of the fire, love,
  Whate'er it finds; destroys.

I will love you like the stars, love,
  Set in the heavenly blue,
That only shine the brighter
  After weeping tears of dew;
Above the wind and fire, love,
  They love the ages through!

And when this life is o'er, love,
  With all its joys and jars,
We'll leave behind the wind and fire
  To wage their boisterous wars—
Then we shall only be, love,
  The nearer to the stars!

                        R. W. RAYMOND

It is not because your heart is mine—mine only—
  Mine alone,
It is not because you choose me weak and lonely
  For your own;
Not because the earth is fairer, and the skies
  Spread above you
Are more radiant for the shining of your eyes—
  That I love you!

It is not because the world's perplexed meaning
  Grows more clear;
And the parapets of heaven, with angels leaning,
  Seem more near;
And Nature sings of praise with all her voices
  Since yours spoke,
Since within my silent heart, that now rejoices,
  Love awoke!

Nay, not even because your hand holds heart and life,
  At your will
Soothing, hushing all its discord, making strife
  Calm and still;
Teaching Trust to fold her wings, nor ever roam
  From her nest;
Teaching Love that her securest, safest home
  Must be rest.

But because this human Love, though true and sweet—
  Yours and mine—
Has been sent by Love more tender, more complete,
  More divine,
That it leads our hearts to rest at last in heaven,
  Far above you;
Do I take you as a gift that God has given—
  And I love you!

ADELAIDE ANNE PROCTER

86 · I'LL NEVER
LOVE THEE MORE

My dear and only love, I pray
   That little world of thee
Be govern'd by no other sway
   But purest monarchy:
For if confusion have a part,
   Which virtuous souls abhor,
I'll call a synod in my heart,
   And never love thee more.

As Alexander I will reign,
   And I will reign alone;
My thoughts did evermore disdain
   A rival on my throne.
He either fears his fate too much,
   Or his deserts are small,
Who dares not put it to the touch,
   To gain or lose it all.

But I will reign and govern still,
   And always give the law,
And have each subject at my will,
   And all to stand in awe:
But 'gainst my batteries if I find
   Thou storm or vex me sore,
As if thou set me as a blind,
   I'll never love thee more.

And in the empire of thy heart,
   Where I should solely be,
If others do pretend a part,
   Or dare to share with me.
Or committees if thou erect,
   Or go on such a score,
I'll smiling mock at thy neglect,
   And never love thee more.

But if no faithless action stain
　　Thy love and constant word,
I'll make thee famous by my pen,
　　And glorious by my sword.
I'll serve thee in such noble ways
　　As ne'er was known before;
I'll deck and crown thy head with bays,
　　And love thee more and more.

JAMES GRAHAM,
MARQUIS OF MONTROSE

87 · LOVE'S PHILOSOPHY

The fountains mingle with the river
　　And the rivers with the ocean,
The winds of heaven mix forever
　　With a sweet emotion;
Nothing in the world is single;
　　All things by a law divine
In one spirit meet and mingle.
　　Why not I with thine?

See the mountain kiss high heaven
　　And the waves clasp one another;
No sister-flower would be forgiven
　　If it disdained its brother;
And the sunlight clasps the earth
　　And the moonbeams kiss the sea:
What is all this sweet work worth
　　If thou kiss not me?

PERCY BYSSHE SHELLEY

88 · BELIEVE ME, IF ALL THOSE ENDEARING YOUNG CHARMS

Believe me, if all those endearing young charms,
   Which I gaze on so fondly today,
Were to change by tomorrow, and fleet in my arms,
   Like fairy gifts, fading away!
Thou wouldst still be ador'd, as this moment thou art,
   Let thy loveliness fade as it will,
And, around the dear ruin, each wish of my heart
   Would entwine itself verdantly still!

It is not, while beauty and youth are thine own,
   And thy cheeks unprofan'd by a tear,
That the fervor and faith of a soul can be known,
   To which time will but make thee more dear!
No, the heart that has truly lov'd, never forgets,
   But as truly loves on to the close,
As the sunflower turns on her god, when he sets,
   The same look which she turn'd when he rose!

THOMAS MOORE

89 · THE DAY RETURNS, MY BOSOM BURNS

The day returns, my bosom burns,
   The blissful day we twa did meet;
Though winter wild in tempest toiled,
   Ne'er summer sun was half sae sweet.
Than a' the pride that loads the tide,
   And crosses o'er the sultry line—
Than kingly robes, and crowns and globes,
   Heaven gave me more; it made thee mine.

While day and night can bring delight,
  Or nature aught of pleasure give—
While joys above my mind can move,
  For thee and thee alone I live;
When that grim foe of life below
  Comes in between to make us part,
The iron hand that breaks our band,
  It breaks my bliss—it breaks my heart.

ROBERT BURNS

90 · A POET TO HIS BELOVED

I bring you with reverent hands
The books of my numberless dreams:
White woman that passion has worn
As the tide wears the dove-gray sands,
And with heart more old than the horn
That is brimmed from the pale fire of time:
White woman with numberless dreams
I bring you my passionate rhyme.

WILLIAM BUTLER YEATS

91 · KISSING HER HAIR

Kissing her hair, I sat against her feet:
Wove and unwove it—wound, and found it sweet;
Made fast there with her hands, drew down her eyes,
Deep as deep flowers, and dreamy like dim skies;
With her own tresses bound, and found her fair—
    Kissing her hair.

Sleep were no sweeter than her face to me—
Sleep of cold sea-bloom under the cold sea:
What pain could get between my face and hers?
What new sweet thing would Love not relish worse?
Unless, perhaps, white Death had kissed me there—
    Kissing her hair.

ALGERNON CHARLES SWINBURNE

92 · LOVE NOT ME FOR COMELY GRACE

Love not me for comely grace,
For my pleasing eye or face,
Nor for any outward part,
No, nor for my constant heart;
    For those may fail or turn to ill,
      So thou and I shall sever;
Keep therefore a true woman's eye,
And love me still, but know not why.
    So hast thou the same reason still
      To dote upon me ever.

AUTHOR UNKNOWN

93 · I LOVE THEE

I love thee—I love thee!
  'Tis all that I can say;
It is my vision in the night,
  My dreaming in the day;
The very echo of my heart,
  The blessing when I pray.
I love thee—I love thee!

I love thee—I love thee!
  Is ever on my tongue.
In all my proudest poesy
  That chorus still is sung;
It is the verdict of my eyes
  Amidst the gay and young:
I love thee—I love thee!
  A thousand maids among.

I love thee—I love thee!
  Thy bright and hazel glance,
The mellow lute upon those lips,
  Whose tender tones entrance.
But most dear heart of hearts, thy
    proofs.
  That still these words enhance!
I love thee—I love thee!
  Whatever be thy chance.

THOMAS HOOD

94 · THE INDIAN SERENADE

I arise from dreams of thee
In the first sweet sleep of night,
When the winds are breathing low,
And the stars are shining bright:
I arise from dreams of thee,
And a spirit in my feet
Hath led me—who knows how?
To thy chamber window, sweet!

AUTHOR UNKNOWN

95 · BEDOUIN LOVE SONG

From the desert I come to thee,
  On a stallion shod with fire;
And the winds are left behind
  In the speed of my desire.
Under thy window I stand,
  And the midnight hears my cry:
I love thee, I love but thee!
  With a love that shall not die:
    Till the sun grows cold,
    And the stars are old,
    And the leaves of the Judgment
    Book unfold!

Look from thy window, and see
  My passion and my pain!
I lie on the sands below,
  And I faint in thy disdain.
Let the night winds touch thy brow
  With the heat of my burning sigh,
And melt thee to hear the vow
  Of a love that shall not die:

Till the sun grows cold,
And the stars are old,
And the leaves of the Judgment
Book unfold!

My steps are nightly driven,
  By the fever in my breast,
To hear from thy lattice breathed
  The word that shall give me rest.
Open the door of thy heart,
  And open thy chamber door,
And my kisses shall teach thy lips
  The love that shall fade no more:
    Till the sun grows cold,
    And the stars are old,
    And the leaves of the Judgment
    Book unfold!
             BAYARD TAYLOR

96 · YES! THOU ART FAIR

Yes! thou art fair, yet be not moved
  To scorn the declaration,
That sometimes I in thee have loved
  My fancy's own creation.

Imagination needs must stir:
  Dear maid, this truth believe,
Minds that have nothing to confer
  Find little to perceive.

Be pleased that nature made thee fit
  To feed my heart's devotion,
By laws to which all forms submit
  In sky, air, earth, and ocean.
           WILLIAM WORDSWORTH

97 · SONNET UPON A STOLEN KISS

Now gentle sleep hath closed up those eyes
Which, waking, kept my boldest thoughts in awe;
And free access unto that sweet lip lies,
From whence I long the rosy breath to draw.
Methinks no wrong it were, if I should steal
From those two melting rubies one poor kiss;
None sees the theft that would the theft reveal,
Nor rob I her of aught what she can miss:
Nay, should I twenty kisses take away,
There would be little sign I would do so;
Why then should I this robbery delay?
O, she may wake, and therewith angry grow!
Well, if she do, I'll back restore that one,
And twenty hundred thousand more for loan.

GEORGE WITHER

98 · AN HOUR WITH THEE

An hour with thee! When earliest day
Dapples with gold the eastern grey,
Oh, what can frame my mind to bear
The toil and turmoil, cark and care,
New griefs, which coming hours unfold,
And sad remembrance of the old?
    One hour with thee.

One hour with thee! When burning June
Waves his red flag at pitch of noon;
What shall repay the faithful swain,
His labor on the sultry plain;
And, more than cave or sheltering bough,
Cool feverish blood and throbbing brow?
    One hour with thee.

One hour with thee! When sun is set,
Oh, what can teach me to forget
The thankless labors of the day;
The hopes, the wishes, flung away;
The increasing wants, and lessening gains,
The master's pride, who scorns my pains?
One hour with thee.

SIR WALTER SCOTT

99 · STANZAS FOR MUSIC

There be none of Beauty's daughters
    With a magic like thee;
And like music on the waters
    Is thy sweet voice to me:
When, as if its sound were causing
The charmèd ocean's pausing,
The waves lie still and gleaming,
And the lull'd winds seem dreaming.

And the midnight moon is weaving
    Her bright chain o'er the deep;
Whose breast is gently heaving,
    As an infant's asleep:
So the spirit bows before thee,
To listen and adore thee;
With a full but soft emotion,
Like the swell of summer's ocean.

GEORGE GORDON, LORD BYRON

100 · I ARISE
FROM DREAMS OF THEE

I arise from dreams of thee
  In the first sweet sleep of night,
When the winds are breathing low,
  And the stars are shining bright.
I arise from dreams of thee,
  And a spirit in my feet
Has led me—who knows how?—
  To thy chamber window, sweet!

The wandering airs they faint
  On the dark, the silent stream—
The champak odors fail
  Like sweet thoughts in a dream;
The nightingale's complaint,
  It dies upon her heart,
As I must die on thine,
  O, beloved as thou art!

O, lift me from the grass!
  I die, I faint, I fail!
Let thy love in kisses rain
  On my lips and eyelids pale.
My cheek is cold and white, alas!
  My heart beats loud and fast:
Oh! press it close to thine again,
  Where it will break at last!
PERCY BYSSHE SHELLEY

101 · I WILL MAKE YOU BROOCHES

I will make you brooches and toys for your delight
Of bird-song at morning and star-shine at night.
I will make a place fit for you and me
Of green days in forest and blue days at sea.

I will make my kitchen, and you shall keep your room,
Where white flows the river and bright blows the broom,
And you shall wash your linen and keep your body white
In rainfall at morning and dewfall at night.

And this shall be for music when no one else is near,
The fine song for singing, the rare song to hear!
That only I remember, that only you admire,
Of the broad road that stretches and the roadside fire.

ROBERT LOUIS STEVENSON

102 · TAKE, O TAKE
THOSE LIPS AWAY

Take, O take those lips away
   That so sweetly were forsworn,
And those eyes, the break of day
   Lights that do mislead the morn;
But my kisses bring again, bring again;
Seals of love, but seal'd in vain, seal'd in vain!

WILLIAM SHAKESPEARE

103 · THE MONOPOLIST

If I were yonder wave, my dear,
　And thou the isle it clasps around,
I would not let a foot come near
　My land of bliss, my fairy ground!

If I were yonder conch of gold,
　And thou the pearl within it placed,
I would not let an eye behold
　The sacred gem my arms embraced!

If I were yonder orange tree,
　And thou the blossom blooming there,
I would not yield a breath of thee,
　To scent the most imploring air!

THOMAS MOORE

104 · WHAT HEAVENLY SMILES!

What heavenly smiles! O Lady mine
Through my very heart they shine;
And, if my brow gives back their light,
Do thou look gladly on the sight;
As the clear Moon with modest pride
　Beholds her own bright beams.
Reflected from the mountain's side
　And from the headlong streams.

WILLIAM WORDSWORTH

105 · THE PASSIONATE SHEPHERD
TO HIS LOVE

Come live with me and be my love,
And we will the pleasures prove
That hills and valleys, dale and field,
And all the craggy mountains yield.

There will we sit upon the rocks
And see the shepherds feed their flocks,
By shallow rivers, to whose falls
Melodious birds sing madrigals.

There will I make thee beds of roses
And a thousand fragrant posies,
A cap of flowers, and a kirtle
Embroider'd all with leaves of myrtle.

A gown made of the finest wool,
Which from our pretty lambs we pull,
Fair linèd slippers for the cold,
With buckles of the purest gold.

A belt of straw and ivy buds
With coral clasps and amber studs:
And if these pleasures may thee move,
Come live with me and be my love.

The shepherd swains shall dance and sing
For thy delight each May morning:
If these delights thy mind may move,
Then live with me and be my love.

CHRISTOPHER MARLOWE

106 · SONNET

O my heart's heart and you who are to me
More than myself myself, God be with you,
  Keep you in strong obedience, leal and true
To him whose noble service setteth free,
Give you all good we see or can foresee,
  Make your joys many and your sorrows few,
  Bless you in what you bear and what you do,
Yea, perfect you as He would have you be.
  So much for you; but what for me, dear friend?
  To love you without stint and all I can
Today, tomorrow, world without an end:
  To love you much, and yet to love you more,
  As Jordan at its flood sweeps either shore;
Since woman is the helpmeet made for man.

CHRISTINA ROSSETTI

107 · WHEN, DEAREST,
I BUT THINK OF THEE

When, dearest, I but think of thee,
Methinks all things that lovely be
  Are present and my soul delighted:
For beauties that from worth arise
Are like the grace of deities,
  Still present with us, tho' unsighted.

Thus while I sit and sigh the day
With all his borrowed lights away,
  Till night's black wings do overtake me,
Thinking on thee, thy beauties then,
As sudden lights do sleepy men,
  So they by their bright rays awake me.

Thus absence dies, and dying proves
No absence can subsist with loves
   That do partake of fair perfection:
Since in the darkest night they may
By love's quick motion find a way
   To see each other by reflection.

The waving sea can with each flood
Bathe some high promont that hath stood
   Far from the main up in the river:
O think not then but love can do
As much! for that's an ocean too,
Which flows not every day, but ever!

                    JOHN SUCKLING

108 · TO LUCASTA, GOING TO THE WARS

Tell me not, sweet, I am unkind,
   That from the nunnery
Of thy chaste breast and quiet mind,
   To war and arms I fly.

True, a new mistress now I chase,
   The first foe in the field;
And with a stronger faith embrace
   A sword, a horse, a shield.

Yet this inconstancy is such
   As you too shall adore;
I could not love thee, dear, so much,
   Lov'd I not honor more.

                    RICHARD LOVELACE

"What will you do, love, when I am going,
With white sail flowing,
   The seas beyond?
What will you do, love, when waves divide us,
And friends may chide us
   For being fond?"
"Though waves divide us, and friends be chiding,
In faith abiding,
   I'll still be true!
And I'll pray for thee on the stormy ocean,
In deep devotion—
   That's what I'll do!"

"What would you do, love, if distant tidings
Thy fond confidings
   Should undermine?
And I, abiding 'neath sultry skies,
Should think other eyes
   Were as bright as thine?"
"Oh, name it not! Though guilt and shame
Were on thy name,
   I'd still be true:
But that heart of thine—should another share it—
I could not bear it!
   What would I do?"

"What would you do, love, when home returning,
With hopes high-burning,
   With wealth for you,
If my bark, which bounded o'er foreign foam,
Should be lost near home—
   Ah! what would you do?"
"So thou wert spared—I'd bless the morrow
In want and sorrow,
   That left me you;

And I'd welcome thee from the wasting billow,
This heart thy pillow—
    That's what I'd do!"

SAMUEL LOVER

110 · REMEMBRANCE

They flee from me that sometime did me seek
With naked foot stalking in my chamber.
I have seen them gentle, tame and meek,
That now are wild and do not remember
That sometime they put themself in danger
To take bread at my hand; and now they range,
Busily seeking with a continual change.

Thanked be fortune, it hath been otherwise
Twenty times better; but once in special,
In thin array after a pleasant guise,
When her loose gown from her shoulders did fall,
And she me caught in her arms long and small;
Therewithal sweetly did me kiss,
And softly said, dear heart, how like you this?

It was no dream: I lay broad waking,
But all is turned through my gentleness
Into a strange fashion of forsaking;
And I have leave to go of her goodness,
And she also to use newfangleness.
But since that I so kindly am served,
I would fain know what she hath deserved.

SIR THOMAS WYATT

Our breath shall intermix, our bosoms bound,
And our veins beat together; and our lips,
With other eloquence than words, eclipse
The soul that burns between them; and the wells
Which boil under our being's inmost cells,
The fountains of our deepest life, shall be
Confused in passion's golden purity,
As mountain springs under the morning sun.
We shall become the same, we shall be one
Spirit within two frames, oh, wherefore two?
One passion in twin hearts, which grows and grew
Till, like two meteors of expanding flame,
Those spheres instinct with it become the same,
Touch, mingle, are transfigured; ever still
Burning, yet ever inconsumable;
In one another's substance finding food,
Light flames too pure and light and unimbued
To nourish their bright lives with baser prey,
Which point to heaven and cannot pass away:
One hope within two wills, one will beneath
Two overshadowing minds, one life, one death,
One heaven, one hell, one immortality,
And one annihilation!

PERCY BYSSHE SHELLEY

I have been here before,
   But when or how I cannot tell:
I know the grass beyond the door,
   The sweet keen smell,
The sighing sound, the lights around the shore.

   You have been mine before—
      How long ago I may not know:
   But just when at that swallow's soar
      Your neck turned so,
Some veil did fall—I knew it all of yore.

   Has this been thus before?
      And shall not thus time's eddying flight
   Still with our lives our love restore
      In death's despite,
And day and night yield one delight once more?

               DANTE GABRIEL ROSSETTI

Among all lovely things my love had been;
Had noted well the stars, all flowers that grew
About her home; but she had never seen
A glowworm, never one, and this I knew.

While riding near her home one stormy night
A single glowworm did I chance to espy;
I gave a fervent welcome to the sight,
And from my horse I leapt; great joy had I.

Upon a leaf the glowworm did I lay,
To bear it with me through the stormy night:
And, as before, it shone without dismay;
Albeit putting forth a fainter light.

When to the dwelling of my love I came,
I went into the orchard quietly;
And left the glowworm, blessing it by name,
Laid safely by itself, beneath a tree.

The whole next day, I hoped, and hoped with fear;
At night the glowworm shone beneath the tree;
I led my Lucy to the spot, "Look here,"
Oh! joy it was for her, and joy for me!

WILLIAM WORDSWORTH

114 · MY QUEEN

He loves not well whose love is bold!
　I would not have thee come too nigh:
The sun's gold would not seem pure gold
　Unless the sun were in the sky;
To take him thence and chain him near
Would make his beauty disappear.

He keeps his state—keep thou in thine,
　And shine upon me from afar!
So shall I bask in light divine,
　That falls from love's own guiding star;
So shall thy eminence be high,
And so my passion shall not die.

But all my life shall reach its hands
　Of lofty longing toward thy face,
And be as one who speechless stands
　In rapture at some perfect grace!
My love, my hope, my all shall be
To look to heaven and look to thee!

Thy eyes shall be the heavenly lights;
　Thy voice the gentle summer breeze,
What time it sways, on moonlit nights,
　The murmuring tops of leafy trees;
And I shall touch thy beauteous form
In June's red roses, rich and warm.

But thou thyself shalt come not down
　From that pure region far above;
But keep thy throne and wear thy crown,
　Queen of my heart and queen of love!
A monarch in thy realm complete,
And I a monarch—at thy feet!

WILLIAM WINTER

115 · A MATCH

If love were what the rose is,
  And I were like the leaf,
Our lives would grow together
In sad or singing weather,
Blown fields or flowerful closes,
  Green pleasure or gray grief;
If love were what the rose is,
  And I were like the leaf.

If I were what the words are,
  And love were like the tune,
With double sound and single
Delight our lips would mingle,
With kisses glad as birds are
  That get sweet rain at noon;
If I were what the words are,
  And love were like the tune.

If you were life, my darling,
  And I your love were death,
We'd shine and snow together
Ere March made sweet the weather
With daffodil and starling
  And hours of fruitful breath;
If you were life, my darling,
  And I your love were death.

If you were thrall to sorrow,
  And I were page to joy,
We'd play for lives and seasons
With loving looks and treasons
And tears of night and morrow
  And laughs of maid and boy;
If you were thrall to sorrow,
  And I were page to joy.

If you were April's lady,
    And I were lord in May,
We'd throw with leaves for hours
And draw for days with flowers,
Till day like night were shady
    And night were bright like day;
If you were April's lady,
    And I were lord in May.

If you were queen of pleasure,
    And I were king of pain,
We'd hunt down love together,
Pluck out his flying-feather,
And teach his feet a measure,
    And find his mouth a rein;
If you were queen of pleasure,
    And I were king of pain.

                ALGERNON CHARLES SWINBURNE

116 · TO ———

Too late I stayed—forgive the crime—
    Unheeded flew the hours:
How noiseless falls the foot of Time
    That only treads on flowers!

And who, with clear account, remarks
    The ebbings of his glass,
When all its sands are diamond sparks,
    That dazzle as they pass?

Ah! who to sober measurement
    Time's happy swiftness brings,
When birds of paradise have lent
    Their plumage to his wings?

                ROBERT WILLIAM SPENCER

117 · ONLY WE

Dream no more that grief and pain
Could such hearts as ours enchain,
Safe from loss and safe from gain,
    Free, as love makes free.

When false friends pass coldly by,
Sigh, in earnest pity, sigh,
Turning thine unclouded eye
    Up from them to me.

Hear not danger's trampling feet,
Feel not sorrow's wintry sleet,
Trust that life is just and meet,
    With mine arm round thee.

Lip on lip, and eye to eye,
Love to love, we live, we die;
No more thou, and no more I,
    We, and only we!
        RICHARD MONCKTON MILNES,
           LORD HOUGHTON

118 · LOVE IN THE WINDS

When I am standing on a mountain crest,
Or hold the tiller in the dashing spray,
My love of you leaps foaming in my breast,
Shouts with the winds and sweeps to their foray;
My heart bounds with the horses of the sea,
And plunges in the wild ride of the night,
Flaunts in the teeth of tempest the large glee
That rides out Fate and welcomes gods to fight.

Ho, love, I laugh aloud for love of you,
Glad that our love is fellow to rough weather—
No fretful orchid hothoused from the dew,
But hale and hardy as the highland heather,
Rejoicing in the wind that stings and thrills,
Comrade of ocean, playmate of the hills.

RICHARD HOVEY

119 · SONNET

I sat with Love upon a woodside well,
  Leaning across the water, I and he;
  Nor ever did he speak nor looked at me,
But touched his lute wherein was audible
The certain secret thing he had to tell:
  Only our mirrored eyes met silently
  In the low wave; and that sound seemed to be
The passionate voice I knew; and my tears fell.

And at their fall, his eyes beneath grew hers;
And with his foot and with his wing-feathers
  He swept the spring that watered my heart's drouth.
Then the dark ripples spread to waving hair,
And as I stopped, her own lips rising there
  Bubbled with brimming kisses at my mouth.

DANTE GABRIEL ROSSETTI

120 · WERE I AS BASE AS IS
THE LOWLY PLAIN

Were I as base as is the lowly plain,
And you, my love, as high as heaven above,
Yet should the thoughts of me your humble swain
Ascend to heaven, in honor of my love.

Were I as high as heaven above the plain,
And you, my love, as humble and as low
As are the deepest bottoms of the main,
Wheresoe'er you were, with you my love should go.

Were you the earth, dear love, and I the skies,
My love should shine on you like to the sun,
And look upon you with ten thousand eyes
Till heaven waxed blind, and till the world were done.

Wheresoe'er I am, below, or else above you,
Wheresoe'er you are, my heart shall truly love you.

JOSHUA SYLVESTER

121 · TO YOU

To you, let snow and roses
And golden locks belong.
These are the world's enslavers,
    Let these delight the throng.
For her of duskier luster
    Whose favor still I wear,
The snow be in her kirtle,
    The rose be in her hair!

The hue of highland rivers
    Careering, full and cool,
From sable on to golden,
    From rapid on to pool—
The hue of heather-honey,
    The hue of honeybees,
Shall tinge her golden shoulder,
    Shall gild her tawny knees.

ROBERT LOUIS STEVENSON

122 · FROM THE ARABIC: AN IMITATION

My faint spirit was sitting in the light
    Of thy looks, my love;
  It panted for thee like the hind at noon
    For the brooks, my love.
The barb whose hoofs outspeed the tempest's flight
    Bore thee far from me;
  My heart, for my weak feet were weary soon,
    Did companion thee.

Ah! fleeter far than fleetest storm or steed,
    Or the death they bear,
  The heart which tender thought clothes like a dove
    With the wings of care;
In the battle, in the darkness, in the need,
    Shall mine cling to thee,
  Nor claim one smile for all the comfort, love,
    It may bring to thee.

PERCY BYSSHE SHELLEY

123 · YOU

God be thanked, the meanest of his creatures
Boasts two soul-sides, one to face the world with,
One to show a woman when he loves her.

This I say of me, but think of you, love!
This to you—yourself, my moon of poets!
Ah, but that's the world's side, there's the wonder,
Thus they see you, praise you, think they know you!
There, in turn I stand with them and praise you—
Out of my own self, I dare to phrase it.

But the best is when I glide from out them,
Cross a step or two of dubious twilight,
Come out on the other side, the novel
Silent silver lights and darks undreamed of
Where I hush and bless myself with silence.

Oh, their Raphael of the dear Madonnas,
Oh, their Dante of the dread Inferno,
Wrote one song—and in my brain I sing it,
Drew one angel—borne, see, on my bosom!

ROBERT BROWNING

Oh, wilt thou have my hand, dear, to lie along
    in thine?
As a little stone in a running stream, it seems to
    lie and pine.
Now drop the poor pale hand, dear, unfit to plight
    with thine.

Oh, wilt thou have my cheek, dear, drawn closer
    to thine own?
My cheek is white, my cheek is worn, by many
    a tear run down.
Now leave a little space, dear, lest it should wet
    thine own.

Oh, must thou have my soul, dear, commingled
    with thy soul?
Red grows the cheek, and warm the hand; the
    part is in the whole:
Nor hands nor cheeks keep separate, when soul
    is joined to soul.

ELIZABETH BARRETT BROWNING

125 · SONNET

Lord of my love, to whom in vassalage
Thy merit hath my duty strongly knit.
To thee I send this written ambassage,
To witness duty, not to show my wit:
Duty so great, which wit so poor as mine
May make seem bare, in wanting words to show it,
But that I hope some good conceit of thine
In thy soul's thought, all naked, will bestow it
Till whatsoever star that guides my moving,
Points on me graciously with fair aspect,
And puts apparel on my tatter'd loving,
To show me worthy of thy sweet respect:
  Then may I dare to boast how I do love thee;
  Till then not show my head where thou mayst
   prove me.
WILLIAM SHAKESPEARE

126 · SONNET

Thus can my love excuse the slow offense
Of my dull bearer when from thee I speed:
From where thou art why should I haste me thence?
Till I return, of posting is no need.
O, what excuse will my poor beast then find,
When swift extremity can seem but slow?
Then should I spur, though mounted on the wind,
In winged speed no motion shall I know:
Then can no horse with my desire keep pace;
Therefore desire, of perfect'st love being made,
Shall neigh—no dull flesh—in his fiery race;
But love, for love, thus shall excuse my jade;
  Since from thee going he went willful-slow,
  Towards thee I'll run and give him leave to go.
WILLIAM SHAKESPEARE

127 · SONNET

Not marble, nor the gilded monuments
Of princes, shall outlive this powerful rhyme;
But you shall shine more bright in these contents
Than unswept stone, besmear'd with sluttish time.
When wasteful war shall statues overturn,
And broils root out the work of masonry,
Nor Mars his sword nor war's quick fire shall burn
The living record of your memory.
'Gainst death and all-oblivious enmity
Shall you pace forth; your praise shall still find room
Even in the eyes of all posterity
That wear this world out to the ending doom.
    So, till the judgement that yourself arise,
    You live in this, and dwell in lovers' eyes.
WILLIAM SHAKESPEARE

128 · SONNET

So are you to my thoughts as food to life,
Or as sweet-season'd showers are to the ground;
And for the peace of you I hold such strife
As 'twixt a miser and his wealth is found;
Now proud as an enjoyer, and anon
Doubting the filching age will steal his treasure;
Now counting best to be with you alone,
Then better'd that the world may see my pleasure:
Sometime all full with feasting on your sight,
And by and by clean starved for a look;
Possessing or pursuing no delight,
Save what is had or must from you be took.
    Thus do I pine and surfeit day by day,
    Or gluttoning on all, or all away.
WILLIAM SHAKESPEARE

129 · SONNET

Some glory in their birth, some in their skill,
Some in their wealth, some in their body's force,
Some in their garments, though new-fangled ill;
Some in their hawks and hounds, some in their horse;
And every humor hath his adjunct pleasure,
Wherein it finds a joy above the rest:
But these particulars are not my measure;
All these I better in one general best.
Thy love is better than high birth to me,
Richer than wealth, prouder than garments cost,
Of more delight than hawks or horses be;
And having thee, of all men's pride I boast:
    Wretched in this alone, that thou mayst take
    All this away and me most wretched make.
                            WILLIAM SHAKESPEARE

130 · SONNET

Indeed this very love which is my boast,
And which, when rising up from breast to brow,
Doth crown me with a ruby large enow
To draw men's eyes and prove the inner cost . . .
This love even, all my worth, to the uttermost,
I should not love withal, unless that thou
Hadst set me an example, shown me how,
When first thine earnest eyes with mine were crossed
And love called love. And thus, I cannot speak
Of love even, as a good thing of my own.
Thy soul hath snatched up mine all faint and weak
And placed it by thee on a golden throne—
And that I love (O soul, we must be meek!)
Is by thee only, whom I love alone.
                        ELIZABETH BARRETT BROWNING

When our two souls stand up erect and strong,
Face to face, silent, drawing nigh and nigher,
Until the lengthening wings break into fire
At either curvèd point—what bitter wrong
Can the earth do to us, that we should not long
Be here contented? Think. In mounting higher,
The angels would press on us and aspire
To drop some golden orb of perfect song
Into our deep, dear silence. Let us stay
Rather on earth, beloved—where the unfit
Contrarious moods of men recoil away
And isolate pure spirits, and permit
A place to stand and love in for a day,
With darkness and the death-hour rounding it.

ELIZABETH BARRETT BROWNING

132 · SONNET

I think of thee! My thoughts do twine and bud
About thee, as wild vines, about a tree,
Put out broad leaves, and soon there's nought to see
Except the straggling green which hides the wood.
Yet, O my palm-tree, be it understood
I will not have my thoughts instead of thee
Who art dearer, better! Rather, instantly
Renew thy presence. As a strong tree should,
Rustle thy boughs and set thy trunk all bare,
And let these bands of greenery which insphere thee,
Drop heavily down . . . burst, shattered, everywhere!
Because, in this deep joy to see and hear thee
And breathe within thy shadow a new air,
I do not think of thee—I am too near thee.

ELIZABETH BARRETT BROWNING

133 · SONNET

How do I love thee? Let me count the ways.
I love thee to the depth and breadth and height
My soul can reach, when feeling out of sight
For the ends of being and ideal grace.
I love thee to the level of everyday's
Most quiet need, by sun and candlelight.
I love thee freely, as men strive for right;
I love thee purely, as they turn from praise.
I love thee with the passion put to use
In my old griefs, and with my childhood's faith.
I love thee with a love I seemed to lose
With my lost saints—I love thee with the breath,
Smiles, tears, of all my life!—and, if God choose,
I shall but love thee better after death.

ELIZABETH BARRETT BROWNING

134 · SONNET

Belovèd, thou hast brought me many flowers
Plucked in the garden, all the summer through
And winter, and it seemed as if they grew
In this close room, nor missed the sun and showers.
So, in the like name of that love of ours,
Take back these thoughts which here unfolded too,
And which on warm and cold days I withdrew
From my heart's ground. Indeed, those beds and bowers
Be overgrown with bitter weeds and rue,
And wait thy weeding; yet here's eglantine,
Here's ivy! Take them, as I used to do
Thy flowers, and keep them where they shall not pine.
Instruct thine eyes to keep their colors true,
And tell thy soul, their roots are left in mine.

ELIZABETH BARRETT BROWNING

Stella this day is thirty-four
(We shan't dispute a year or more),
However Stella, be not troubled,
Although thy size and years are doubled,
Since first I saw thee at sixteen
The brightest virgin on the green,
So little is thy form declin'd
Made up so largely in thy mind.
Oh, would it please the gods to split
Thy beauty, size, and years, and wit,
No age could furnish out a pair
Of nymphs so graceful, wise and fair
With half the luster of your eyes,
With half your wit, your years and size:
And then before it grew too late,
How should I beg of gentle Fate
(That either nymph might have her swain)
To split my worship too in twain.

JONATHAN SWIFT

Bid me to live, and I will live
    Thy Protestant to be;
Or bid me love, and I will give
    A loving heart to thee.

A heart as soft, a heart as kind,
    A heart as sound and free,
As in the whole world thou canst find,
    That heart I'll give to thee.

Bid that heart stay, and it will stay
    To honor thy decree;
Or bid it languish quite away,
    And't shall do so for thee.

Bid me to weep, and I will weep,
    While I have eyes to see;
And having none, yet I will keep
    A heart to weep for thee.

Thou art my life, my love, my heart,
    The very eyes of me;
And hast command of every part,
    To live and die for thee.
                ROBERT HERRICK

137 · TO HIS LADY JOAN, OF FLORENCE

Flowers hast thou in thyself, and foliage,
    And what is good, and what is glad to see;
The sun is not so bright as thy visage;
    All is stark naught when one hath look'd on thee;

There is not such a beautiful personage
   Anywhere on the green earth verily;
If one fear love, thy bearing sweet and sage
   Comforteth him, and no more fear hath he.
Thy lady friends and maidens ministering
   Are all, for love of thee, much to my taste:
And much I pray them that in everything
   They honor thee even as thou meritest,
And have thee in their gentle harboring:
   Because among them all thou art the best.

GUIDO CAVALCANTI
translated by Dante Gabriel Rossetti

138 · A RAPTURE CONCERNING HIS LADY

Who is she coming, whom all gaze upon,
   Who makes the air all tremulous with light,
And at whose side is Love himself? that none
   Dare speak, but each man's sighs are infinite.
Ah me! how she looks round from left to right,
   Let Love discourse: I may not speak thereon.
   Lady she seems of such high benison
As makes all others graceless in men's sight.
The honor which is hers cannot be said;
   To whom are subject all things virtuous,
     While all things beauteous own her deity.
Ne'er was the mind of man so nobly led
   Nor yet was such redemption granted us
     That we should ever know her perfectly.

GUIDO CALVACANTI
translated by Dante Gabriel Rossetti

Though the day of my destiny's over,
  And the star of my fate hath declined,
Thy soft heart refused to discover
  The faults which so many could find;
Though thy soul with my grief was acquainted,
  It shrunk not to share it with me,
And the love which my spirit hath painted
  It never hath found but in *thee*.

Then when nature around me is smiling,
  The last smile which answers to mine,
I do not believe it beguiling,
  Because it reminds me of thine;
And when winds are at war with the ocean,
  As the breasts I believed in with me.
If their billows excite an emotion,
  It is that they bear me from *thee*.

Though the rock of my last hope is shiver'd,
  And its fragments are sunk in the wave,
Though I feel that my soul is deliver'd
  To pain—it shall not be its slave.
There is many a pang to pursue me:
  They may crush, but they shall not contemn—
They may torture, but shall not subdue me—
  'Tis of *thee* that I think—not of them.

Though human, thou didst not deceive me,
  Though woman, thou didst not forsake,
Though loved, thou forborest to grieve me,
  Though slander'd, thou never couldst shake—
Though trusted, thou didst not disclaim me,
  Though parted, it was not to fly,
Though watchful, 'twas not to defame me,
  Nor, mute, that the world might belie.

Yet I blame not the world, nor despise it,
   Nor the war of the many with one—
If my soul was not fitted to prize it,
   'Twas folly not sooner to shun:
And if dearly that error hath cost me,
   And more than I once could foresee,
I have found that, whatever it lost me,
   It could not deprive me of *thee*.

From the wreck of the past, which hath perish'd,
   Thus much I at least may recall,
It hath taught me that what I most cherish'd
   Deserved to be dearest of all:
In the desert a fountain is springing,
   In the wide waste there still is a tree,
And a bird in the solitude singing,
   Which speaks to my spirit of *thee*.
             GEORGE GORDON, LORD BYRON

140 · TO ———

Let other bards of angels sing,
   Bright suns without a spot;
But thou art no such perfect thing:
   Rejoice that thou art not!

Heed not tho' none should call thee fair:
   So, Mary, let it be
If naught in loveliness compare
   With what thou art to me.

True beauty dwells in deep retreats,
   Whose veil is unremoved
Till heart with heart in concord beats,
   And the lover is beloved.
             WILLIAM WORDSWORTH

141 · I LOVE MY JEAN

Of a' the airts the wind can blaw,
  I dearly like the west;
For there the bonnie lassie lives,
  The lassie I lo'e best.
There wild woods grow, and rivers row,
  And monie a hill's between;
But day and night my fancy's flight
  Is ever wi' my Jean.

I see her in the dewy flowers,
  I see her sweet and fair;
I hear her in the tunefu' birds,
  I hear her charm the air;
There's not a bonnie flower that springs
  By fountain, shaw, or green;
There's not a bonnie bird that sings,
  But minds me of my Jean.

ROBERT BURNS

142 · TO ELECTRA

I dare not ask a kiss,
  I dare not beg a smile,
Lest having that, or this,
  I might grow proud the while.

No, no, the utmost share
  Of my desire shall be,
Only to kiss that air
  That lately kissèd thee.

ROBERT HERRICK

When Love with unconfinèd wings
   Hovers within my gates,
And my divine Althea brings
   To whisper at the grates;
When I lie tangled in her hair
   And fetter'd to her eye,
The birds that wanton in the air
   Know no such liberty.

When flowing cups run swiftly round
   With no allaying Thames,
Our careless heads with roses crown'd,
   Our hearts with loyal flames;
When thirsty grief in wine we steep,
   When healths and draughts go free—
Fishes that tipple in the deep
   Know no such liberty.

When, linnetlike confinèd, I
   With shriller throat shall sing
The sweetness, mercy, majesty
   And glories of my king;
When I shall voice aloud how good
   He is, how great should be,
Enlarged winds, that curl the flood,
   Know no such liberty.

Stone walls do not a prison make,
   Nor iron bars a cage;
Minds innocent and quiet take
   That for an hermitage:
If I have freedom in my love
   And in my soul am free,
Angels alone, that soar above,
   Enjoy such liberty.

RICHARD LOVELACE

144 · TO ELLEN

Oh! might I kiss those eyes of fire,
A million scarce would quench desire:
Still would I steep my lips in bliss,
And dwell an age on every kiss;
Nor then my soul should sated be,
Still would I kiss and cling to thee:
Nought should my kiss from thine dissever;
Still would we kiss, and kiss forever,
E'en though the numbers did exceed
The yellow harvest's countless seed.
To part would be a vain endeavor:
Could I desist? Ah, never—never!

GEORGE GORDON, LORD BYRON

145 · LAURA'S SONG

Alas! who knows or cares, my love,
    If our love live or die—
If thou thy frailty, sweet, should prove,
    Or my soul thine deny?
Yet merging sorrow in delight,
Love's dream disputes our devious night.

None know, sweet love, nor care a thought
    For our heart's vague desire,
Nor if our longing come to nought,
    Or burn in aimless fire;
Let them alone, we'll waste no sighs:
Cling closer, love, and close thine eyes!

OLIVER MADOX BROWN

146 · THOU HAST SWORN BY THY GOD, MY JEANIE

Thou hast sworn by thy God, my Jeanie,
  By that pretty white hand o' thine,
And by a' the lowing stars in heaven,
  That thou wad aye be mine!
And I hae sworn by my God, my Jeanie,
  And by that kind heart o' thine,
By a' the stars sown thick owre heaven,
  That thou shalt aye be mine!

Then foul fa' the hands that wad loose sic bands,
  And the heart that wad part sic luve!
But there's nae hand can loose the band,
  But the finger o' God abuve.
Though the wee, wee cot maun be my bield,
  An' my claithing ne'er sae mean,
I wad lap me up rich i' the faulds o' luve—
  Heaven's armfu' o' my Jean!

Her white arm wad be a pillow to me,
  Fu' safter than the down;
An' Luve wad winnow owre us his kind, kind wings,
  An' sweetly I'd sleep, an' soun'.
Come here to me, thou lass, o' my luve!
  Come here and kneel wi' me!
The morn is fu' o' the presence o' God,
  An' I canna pray without thee.

The morn-wind is sweet 'mang the beds o' new flowers,
  The wee birds sing kindlie an' hie;
Our gudeman leans owre his kail-yard dike,
  And a blythe auld bodie is he.
The Book maun be ta'en whan the carle come hame,
  Wi' the holie psalmodie;
And thou maun speak o' me to thy God,
  And I will speak o' thee.

ALLAN CUNNINGHAM

147 · ROBIN ADAIR

What's this dull town to me?
  Robin's not near—
He whom I wished to see,
  Wished for to hear;
Where's all the joy and mirth
Made life a heaven on earth,
O, they're all fled with thee,
  Robin Adair!

What made the assembly shine?
  Robin Adair:
What made the ball so fine?
  Robin was there:
What, when the play was o'er,
What made my heart so sore?
O, it was parting with
  Robin Adair!

But now thou art far from me,
  Robin Adair;
But now I never see
  Robin Adair;
Yet him I loved so well
Still in my heart shall dwell;
O, I can ne'er forget
  Robin Adair!

Welcome on shore again,
  Robin Adair!
Welcome once more again,
  Robin Adair!
I feel thy trembling hand;
Tears in thy eyelids stand,
To greet thy native land,
  Robin Adair.

Long I ne'er saw thee, love,
  Robin Adair;
Still I prayed for thee, love,
  Robin Adair;
When thou wert far at sea,
Many made love to me,
But still I thought on thee,
  Robin Adair.

Come to my heart again,
  Robin Adair;
Never to part again,
  Robin Adair;
And if thou still art true,
I will be constant too,
And will wed none but you,
  Robin Adair!
                LADY CAROLINE KEPPEL

148 · TO A LADY ASKING HIM HOW LONG HE WOULD LOVE HER

It is not, Celia, in our power
  To say how long our love will last;
It may be we within this hour
  May lose those joys we now do taste:
The blessed, that immortal be,
From change in love are only free.

Then since we mortal lovers are,
  Ask not how long our love will last;
But while it does, let us take care
  Each minute be with pleasure passed:
Were it not madness to deny
To live because we're sure to die?
                GEORGE ETHEREGE

Turn I my looks unto the skies,
Love with his arrows wounds mine eyes:
If so I gaze upon the ground,
Love then in every flower is found:
Search I the shade to fly my pain,
He meets me in the shade again:
Wend I to walk in secret grove,
Ev'n there I melt with sacred Love:
If so I bain me in the spring,
Ev'n on the brink I hear him sing:
If so I meditate alone,
He will be partner of my moan:
If so I mourn, he weeps with me,
And where I am, there will he be.
When as I talk of Rosalind,
The god from coyness waxeth kind,
And seems in selfsame flames to fry,
Because he loves as well as I;
Sweet Rosalind, for pity, rue!
For why than love I am more true:
He, if he speed, will quickly fly;
But in thy love I live and die.

THOMAS LODGE

150 · CONCERNING LUCY

When Lucy draws her mantle round her face,
So sweeter than all else she is to see,
That hence unto the hills there lives not he
Whose whole soul would not love her for her grace.
Then seems she like a daughter of some race
That holds high rule in France or Germany:

And a snake's head stricken off suddenly
Throbs never as then throbs my heart to embrace
Her body in these arms, even were she loth;
    To kiss her lips, to kiss her cheeks, to kiss
        The lids of her two eyes which are two flames.
    Yet what my heart so longs for, my heart blames:
For surely sorrow might be bred from this
Where some man's patient love abides its growth.

GUIDO GUINICELLI
translated by Dante Gabriel Rossetti

151 · HE WILL PRAISE HIS LADY

Yea, let me praise my lady whom I love,
    Likening her unto the lily and rose:
    Brighter than morning star her visage glows;
She is beneath even as her saint above:
She is as the air in summer which God wove
    Of purple and of vermilion glorious;
    As gold and jewels richer than man knows.
Love's self, being love for her, must holier prove.
Ever as she walks she hath a sober grace,
    Making bold men abash'd and good men glad;
    If she delight thee not, thy heart must err.
No man dare look on her his thoughts being base:
    Nay, let me say even more than I have said;
    No man could think base thoughts who look'd on
        her.

GUIDO GUINICELLI
translated by Dante Gabriel Rossetti

152 · TO CELIA

Drink to me only with thine eyes,
    And I will pledge with mine;
Or leave a kiss but in the cup
    And I'll not look for wine.
The thirst that from the soul doth rise
    Doth ask a drink divine;
But might I of Jove's nectar sup,
    I would not change for thine.

I sent thee late a rosy wreath,
    Not so much honoring thee
As giving it a hope that there
    It could not wither'd be;
But thou thereon didst only breathe
    And sent'st it back to me;
Since when it grows, and smells, I swear,
    Not of itself but thee!

BEN JONSON

153 · MY CHOICE

Shall I tell you whom I love?
    Hearken then awhile to me;
And if such a woman move
    As I now shall versify,
Be assured 't is she or none,
That I love, and love alone.

Nature did her so much right
    As she scorns the help of art.
In as many virtues dight
    As e'er yet embraced a heart.

So much good so truly tried,
Some for less were deified.

Wit she hath, without desire
   To make known how much she hath;
And her anger flames no higher
   Than may fitly sweeten wrath.
Full of pity as may be,
Though perhaps not so to me.

Reason masters every sense,
   And her virtues grace her birth;
Lovely as all excellence,
   Modest in her most of mirth.
Likelihood enough to prove
Only worth could kindle love.

Such she is; and if you know
   Such a one as I have sung;
Be she brown, or fair, or so
   That she be but somewhat young;
Be assured 'tis she, or none,
That I love, and love alone.

WILLIAM BROWNE

Go, lovely rose—
Tell her that wastes her time and me,
 That now she knows,
When I resemble her to thee,
How sweet and fair she seems to be.

 Tell her that's young,
And shuns to have her graces spied,
 That hadst thou sprung
In deserts where no men abide,
Thou must have uncommended died.

 Small is the worth
Of beauty from the light retired:
 Bid her come forth,
Suffer herself to be desired,
And not blush so to be admired.

 Then die! that she
The common fate of all things rare
 May read in thee;
How small a part of time they share
That are so wondrous sweet and fair!

EDMUND WALLER

155 · SURRENDER

Doubt me, my dim companion!
Why, God would be content
With but a fraction of the love
Poured thee without a stint.
The whole of me, forever,
What more the woman can—
Say quick, that I may dower thee
With last delight I own!

It cannot be my spirit,
For that was thine before;
I ceded all of dust I knew—
What opulence the more
Had I, a humble maiden,
Whose farthest of degree
Was that she might,
Some distant heaven,
Dwell timidly with thee!
EMILY DICKINSON

Sweet nea! for your lovely sake
  I weave these rambling numbers,
Because I've lain an hour awake,
  And can't compose my slumbers;
Because your beauty's gentle light
  Is round my pillow beaming,
And flings, I know not why, tonight,
  Some witchery round my dreaming.

Because we've passed some joyous days,
  And danced some merry dances;
Because we love old Beaumont's plays,
  And old Froissart's romances!
Because whene'er I hear your words,
  Some pleasant feeling lingers;
Because I think your heart has chords
  That vibrate to your fingers!

Because you've got those long, soft curls
  I've sworn should deck my goddess;
Because you're not, like other girls,
  All bustle, blush, and bodice!
Because your eyes are deep and blue,
  Your fingers long and rosy;
Because a little child and you
  Would make one's home so cozy.

Because your little tiny nose
  Turns up so pert and funny;
Because I know you choose your beaux
  More for their mirth than money;
Because I think you'd rather twirl
  A waltz, with me to guide you,
Than talk small nonsense with an earl,
  And a coronet beside you!

Because you don't object to walk,
　　And are not given to fainting;
Because you have not learnt to talk
　　Of flowers and Poonah-painting;
Because I think you'd scarce refuse
　　To sew one on a button;
Because I know you'd sometimes choose
　　To dine on simple mutton!

Because I think I'm just so weak
　　As, some of those fine morrows,
To ask you if you'll let me speak,
　　My story—and *my* sorrows;
Because the rest's a simple thing,
　　A matter quickly over,
A church—a priest—a sigh—a ring—
　　And a chaise and four to Dover.

EDWARD FITZGERALD

The clouds have deepened o'er the night
  Till, through the dark profound,
The moon is but a stain of light
  And all the stars are drowned;
And all the stars are drowned, my love,
  And all the skies are drear;
But what care we for light above,
  If light of love is here?

The wind is like a wounded thing
  That beats about the gloom
With baffled breast and drooping wing
  And wail of deepest doom;
And wail of deepest doom, my love;
  But what have we to fear
From night, or rain, or winds above,
  With love and laughter here?

JAMES WHITCOMB RILEY

I left you in the morning,
And in the morning glow
You walked a way beside me
To make me sad to go.
Do you know me in the gloaming,
Gaunt and dusty gray with roaming?
Are you dumb because you know me not,
Or dumb because you know?

All for me? And not a question
For the faded flowers gay
That could take me from beside you
For the ages of a day?
They are yours, and be the measure
Of their worth for you to treasure,
The measure of the little while
That I've been long away.

ROBERT FROST

159 · SONNET

He touched me, so I live to know
That such a day, permitted so,
   I groped upon his breast.
It was a boundless place to me,
And silenced, as the awful sea
   Puts minor streams to rest.

And now, I'm different from before,
As if I breathed superior air,
   Or brushed a royal gown;
My feet, too, that had wandered so,
My gypsy face transfigured now
   To tenderer renown.

EMILY DICKINSON

With

Eyes

of

Love

She walks in beauty, like the night
Of cloudless climes and starry skies,
And all that's best of dark and bright
Meets in her aspect and her eyes,
Thus mellow'd to that tender light
Which heaven to gaudy day denies.

One shade the more, one ray the less
Had half impair'd the nameless grace
Which waves in every raven tress
Or softly lightens o'er her face,
Where thoughts serenely sweet express
How pure, how dear their dwelling-place.

And on that cheek and o'er that brow
So soft, so calm, yet eloquent,
The smiles that win, the tints that glow
But tell of days in goodness spent—
A mind at peace with all below,
A heart whose love is innocent.

GEORGE GORDON, LORD BYRON

161 · JULIA

Some asked me where the rubies grew,
    And nothing did I say,
But with my finger pointed to
    The lips of Julia.

Some asked how pearls did grow, and where;
    Then spake I to my girl,
To part her lips and show me there
    The quarelets of pearl.

One asked me where the roses grew;
    I bade him not go seek,
But forthwith bade my Julia show
    A bud in either cheek.

ROBERT HERRICK

162 · UPON THE NIPPLES
OF JULIA'S BREAST

Have ye beheld (with much delight)
A red rose peeping through a white?
Or else a cherry (double grac'd)
Within a lily? Center plac'd?
Or ever mark'd the pretty beam,
A strawberry shows, half drown'd in cream?
Or seen rich rubies blushing through
A pure smooth pearl, and orient too?
So like to this, nay all the rest,
Is each neat niplet of her breast.

ROBERT HERRICK

163 · UPON JULIA'S CLOTHES

When as in silks my Julia goes,
Then, then (me thinks) how sweetly flows
The liquefaction of her clothes.

Next, when I cast mine eyes and see
That brave vibration each way free,
O how that glittering taketh me!

ROBERT HERRICK

164 · TO HELEN

Helen, thy beauty is to me
  Like those Nicæan barks of yore
That gently, o'er a perfumed sea,
  The weary, wayworn wanderer bore
  To his own native shore.

On desperate seas long wont to roam,
  Thy hyacinth hair, thy classic face,
Thy Naiad airs have brought me home
  To the glory that was Greece
  And the grandeur that was Rome.

Lo! in yon brilliant window niche
  How statuelike I see thee stand,
The agate lamp within thy hand!
  Ah, Psyche, from the regions which
  Are Holy Land!

EDGAR ALLAN POE

165 · RUTH

She stood breast high amid the corn,
Clasped by the golden light of morn,
Like the sweetheart of the sun,
Who many a glowing kiss had won.

On her cheek an autumn flush,
Deeply ripened; such a blush
In the midst of brown was born,
Like red poppies grown with corn.

Round her eyes her tresses fell,
Which were blackest none could tell,
But long lashes veiled a light,
That had else been all too bright.

And her hat, with shady brim,
Made her tressy forehead dim—
Thus she stood amid the stooks,
Praising God with sweetest looks:

Sure, I said, heaven did not mean,
Where I reap thou shouldst but glean,
Lay they sheaf adown and come,
Share my harvest and my home.

Thomas Hood

166 · TO MISS M———

Sweet gentle angel, not that I aspire
　　To win they favor, though ambition raise
　　My wishes high, I wake anew my lays;
　　But that thine image may adorn my lyre
With beauty, more than fancy could inspire!
　　As, when behind the silver clouds she strays,
　　The moon peeps through, and sheds a mellow blaze,
　　Till woods, hills, valleys, with enchantment fire;
So does they soul, though pent in mortal mold,
　　Break through the brightened veil; illume thy form;
With softened lights each varied feature warm;
　　And in thine eyes such fairy radiance hold,
That on each object round they beam a magic charm.

Sir Samuel Egerton Brydges

167 · FANNIE

Fannie has the sweetest foot
Ever in a gaiter boot!
And the hoyden knows it,
And, of course, she shows it—
Not the knowledge, but the foot—
Yet with such a modest grace,
Never seems it out of place,
    Ah, there are not many
      Half so sly, or sad, or mad,
    Or wickeder than Fannie.

Fannie has the blackest hair
   Of any of the village girls;
It does not shower on her neck
   In silken or coquettish curls.
It droops in folds around her brow,
   As clouds, at night, around the moon,
Looped with lilies here and there,
   In many a dangerous festoon.
And Fannie wears a gipsy hat,
Saucily—yes, all of that!
    Ah, there are not many
      Half so sly, or sad, or mad,
    Or wickeder than Fannie.

Fannie wears an open dress—
   Ah! the charming chemisette!
Half concealing, half revealing
   Something far more charming yet.
Fannie drapes her breast with lace,
As one would drape a costly vase
To keep away mischievous flies;
But lace can't keep away one's eyes,
For every time her bosom heaves,
    Ah, it peepeth through it;

Yet Fannie looks the while as if
  Never once she knew it.
    Ah, there are not many
      Half so sly, or sad, or mad,
    Or innocent as Fannie.

Fannie lays her hand in mine;
  Fannie speaks with naïveté,
Fannie kisses me, she does!
  In her own coquettish way.
Then softly speaks and deeply sighs,
With angels nestled in her eyes.
In the merrie month of May,
Fannie swears sincerely
She will be my own, my wife,
And love me dearly, dearly
Ever after all her life.
    Ah, there are not many
      Half so sly, or sad, or mad,
    As my true-hearted Fannie.
                THOMAS BAILEY ALDRICH

In Celia's face a question did arise:
Which were more beautiful, her lips or eyes.
"We," said the eyes, "send forth those pointed darts
Which pierce the hardest adamantine hearts."
"From us," replied the lips, "proceed those blisses
Which lovers reap by kind words and sweet kisses."
Then wept the eyes, and from their springs did pour
Of liquid oriental pearl a shower,
Whereat the lips, moved with delight and pleasure,
Through a sweet smile unlocked their pearly treasure,
And bade Love judge whether did add more grace
Weeping or smiling pearls to Celia's face.

THOMAS CAREW

169 · SONNET

My lady carries love within her eyes;
   All that she looks on is made pleasanter;
   Upon her path men turn to gaze at her;
He whom she greeteth feels his heart to rise,
And droops his troubled visage, full of sighs,
   And of his evil heart is then aware:
   Hate loves, and pride becomes a worshipper.
O women, help to praise her in somewise.
Humbleness, and the hope that hopeth well,
   By speech of hers into the mind are brought,
   And who beholds is blessed oftenwhiles.
   The look she hath when she a little smiles
   Cannot be said, nor holden in the thought;
'Tis such a new and gracious miracle.

DANTE ALIGHIERI
translated by Dante Gabriel Rossetti

170 · SONNET

For certain he hath seen all perfectness
    Who among other ladies hath seen mine:
    They that go with her humbly should combine
To thank their God for such peculiar grace.
So perfect is the beauty of her face
    That it begets in no wise any sign
    Of envy, but draws round her a clear line
Of love, and blessed faith, and gentleness.
Merely the sight of her makes all things bow:
    Not she herself alone is holier
        Than all; but hers, through her, are raised above.
From all her acts such lovely graces flow
    That truly one may never think of her
        Without a passion of exceeding love.

> DANTE ALIGHIERI,
> *translated by Dante Gabriel Rossetti*

171 · A VISION OF BEAUTY

It was a beauty that I saw—
    So pure, so perfect, as the frame
    Of all the universe were lame
To that one figure, could I draw,
Or give least line of it a law:
    A skein of silk without a knot!
A fair march made without a halt!
A curious form without a fault!
    A printed book without a blot!
    All beauty!—and without a spot.

> BEN JONSON

Her dimpled cheeks are pale;
She's a lily of the vale,
      Not a rose.
In a muslin or a lawn
She is fairer than the dawn
      To her beaux.

Her boots are slim and neat—
She is vain about her feet,
      It is said.
She amputates her r's,
But her eyes are like the stars
      Overhead.

On a balcony at night,
With a fleecy cloud of white
      Round her hair—
Her grace, ah, who could paint?
She would fascinate a saint,
      I declare.

'Tis a matter of regret,
She's a bit of a coquette,
      Whom I sing:
On her cruel path she goes
With a half a dozen beaux
      To her string.

But let all that pass by,
As her maiden moments fly,
      Dew-empearled;
When she marries, on my life,
She will make the dearest wife
      In the world.
                    SAMUEL MINTURN PECK

173 · O, FAIREST OF
THE RURAL MAIDS!

O, fairest of the rural maids!
Thy birth was in the forest shades;
Green boughs, and glimpses of the sky,
Were all that met thine infant eye.

Thy sports, thy wanderings, when a child,
Were ever in the sylvan wild,
And all the beauty of the place
Is in thy heart and on thy face.

The twilight of the trees and rocks
Is in the light shade of thy locks;
Thy step is as the wind, that weaves
Its playful way among the leaves.

Thine eyes are springs, in whose serene
And silent waters heaven is seen;
Their lashes are the herbs that look
On their young figures in the brook.

The forest depths, by foot unpressed,
Are not more sinless than they breast;
The holy peace, that fills the air
Of those calm solitudes, is there.

WILLIAM CULLEN BRYANT

174 · SONNET

My lady's presence makes the roses red,
Because to see her lips they blush for shame;
The lily's leaves, for envy, pale became,
For her white hands in them this envy bred.
The marigold the leaves abroad doth spread,
Because the sun's and her power is the same;
The violet of purple color came,
Dyed in the blood she made my heart to shed.
In brief, all flowers from her their virtue take;
From her sweet breath their sweet smells do proceed;
The living heat which her eyebeams do make
Warmeth the ground, and quickeneth the seed.
The rain, wherewith she watereth the flowers,
Falls from mine eyes, which she dissolves in showers.

HENRY CONSTABLE

175 · THERE IS A GARDEN
IN HER FACE

There is a garden in her face,
　　Where roses and white lilies grow;
A heavenly paradise is that place,
　　Wherein all pleasant fruits do grow;
There cherries grow that none may buy
Till cherry ripe themselves do cry.

Those cherries fairly do enclose
　　Of orient pearl a double row,
Which, when her lovely laughter shows,
　　They look like rosebuds fill'd with snow;
Yet them no peer nor prince may buy
Till cherry ripe themselves do cry.

Her eyes like angels watch them still,
 Her brows like bended bows do stand,
Threatening with piercing frowns to kill
 All that approach with eye or hand
These sacred cherries to come nigh,
Till cherry ripe themselves do cry.

RICHARD ALLISON

176 · THE GARDEN OF BEAUTY

Coming to kiss her lips (such grace I found),
Me seem'd I smelt a garden of sweet flow'rs,
That dainty odors from them threw around,
For damsels fit to deck their lovers' bow'rs.
Her lips did smell like unto gilliflowers,
Her ruddy cheeks like unto roses red,
Her snowy brows like budded bellamoures,
Her lovely eyes like pinks but newly spread,
Her goodly bosom like a strawberry bed,
Her neck like to a bunch of cullambines,
Her breast like lilies ere their leaves be shed,
Her nipples like young blossom'd jessamines:
Such fragrant flow'rs do give most odorous smell,
But her sweet odor did them all excel.

EDMUND SPENSER

177 · IT IS NOT BEAUTY
I DEMAND

It is not beauty I demand,
  A crystal brow, the moon's despair,
Nor the snow's daughter, a white hand,
  Nor mermaid's yellow pride of hair.

Tell me not of your starry eyes,
  Your lips that seem on roses fed,
Your breasts where Cupid trembling lies,
  Nor sleeps for kissing of his bed.

A bloomy pair of vermeil cheeks,
  Like Hebe's in her ruddiest hours,
A breath that softer music speaks
  Than summer winds a-wooing flowers.

These are but gauds; nay, what are lips?
  Coral beneath the ocean-stream,
Whose brink when your adventurer sips
  Full oft he perisheth on them.

And what are cheeks but ensigns oft
  That wave hot youth to fields of blood?
Did Helen's breast though ne'er so soft,
  Do Greece or Ilium any good?

Eyes can with baleful ardor burn,
  Poison can breath that erst perfumed,
There's many a white hand holds an urn
  With lovers' hearts to dust consumed.

For crystal brows—there's naught within,
  They are but empty cells for pride;
He who the Syren's hair would win
  Is mostly strangled in the tide.

Give me, instead of beauty's bust,
  A tender heart, a loyal mind,
Which with temptation I could trust,
  Yet never linked with error find.

One in whose gentle bosom I
  Could pour my secret heart of woes,
Like the care-burdened honey-fly
  That hides his murmurs in the rose.
                          GEORGE DARLEY

178 · HE COMPARES ALL THINGS
WITH HIS LADY,
AND FINDS THEM WANTING

Beauty in woman; the high will's decree;
  Fair knighthood arm'd for manly exercise;
  The pleasant song of birds; love's soft replies;
The strength of rapid ships upon the sea;
The serene air when light begins to be;
  The white snow, without wind that falls and lies;
  Fields of all flower; the place where waters rise;
Silver and gold; azure in jewelry:
Weigh'd against these, the sweet and quiet worth
  Which my dear lady cherishes at heart
    Might seem a little matter to be shown;
  Being truly, over these, as much apart
As the whole heaven is greater than this earth.
  All good to kindred natures cleaveth soon.
                          GUIDO CAVALCANTI
                translated by Dante Gabriel Rossetti

179 · SONNET

Not from the stars do I my judgement pluck;
And yet methinks I have astronomy,
But not to tell of good or evil luck,
Of plagues, of dearths, or seasons' quality;
Nor can I fortune to brief minutes tell,
Pointing to each his thunder, rain and wind,
Or say with princes if it shall go well,
By oft predict that I in heaven find:
But from thine eyes my knowledge I derive,
And, constant stars, in them I read such art,
As truth and beauty shall together thrive,
If from thyself to store thou wouldst convert;
    Or else of thee this I prognosticate:
    Thy end is truth's and beauty's doom and date.

WILLIAM SHAKESPEARE

180 · SONNET

Shall I compare thee to a summer's day?
Thou art more lovely and more temperate:
Rough winds do shake the darling buds of May,
And summer's lease hath all too short a date:
Sometime too hot the eye of heaven shines,
And often is his gold complexion dimm'd;
And every fair from fair sometime declines,
By chance or nature's changing course untrimm'd;
But thy eternal summer shall not fade,
Nor lose possession of that fair thou owest;
Nor shall Death brag thou wander'st in his shade,
When in eternal lines to time thou grow'st;
    So long as men can breathe, or eyes can see,
    So long lives this, and this gives life to thee.

WILLIAM SHAKESPEARE

181 · SONNET

When in the chronicle of wasted time
I see descriptions of the fairest wights,
And beauty making beautiful old rhyme
In praise of ladies dead and lovely knights,
Then, in the blazon of sweet beauty's best,
Of hand, of foot, of lip, of eye, of brow,
I see their antique pen would have express'd
Even such a beauty as you master now.
So all their praises are but prophecies
Of this our time, all you prefiguring;
And, for they look'd but with divining eyes,
They had not skill enough your worth to sing:
    For we, which now behold these present days,
    Have eyes to wonder, but lack tongues to praise.

WILLIAM SHAKESPEARE

182 · SONNET

My mistress' eyes are nothing like the sun;
Coral is far more red than her lips' red:
If snow be white, why then her breasts are dun;
If hairs be wires, black wires grow on her head.
I have seen roses damask'd, red and white,
But no such roses see I in her cheeks;
And in some perfumes is there more delight
Than in the breath that from my mistress reeks.
I love to hear her speak, yet well I know
That music hath a far more pleasing sound:
I grant I never saw a goddess go,
My mistress, when she walks, treads on the ground:
    And yet, by heaven, I think my love as rare
    As any she belied with false compare.

WILLIAM SHAKESPEARE

183 · YOUR TWO EYES

Your two eyes will slay me suddenly,
I may the beauty of them not sustain,
So woundeth it throughout my hertè keen;

And but your word will healen hastily
My hertès woundè, while that it is green,
  Your two eyes would slay me suddenly,
  I may the beauty of them not sustain.

Upon my trouthe, I tell you faithfully
That you be of my life and death the queen;
For with my death the trouthè shall be seen.
  Your two eyes will slay me suddenly,
  I may the beauty of them not sustain,
  So woundeth it through all my hertè keen.
                                GEOFFREY CHAUCER

184 · MY LADY'S EYES

Mistress, since you so much desire
To know the place of Cupid's fire,
In your fair shrine that flame doth rest,
Yet never harbored in your breast.

It bides not in your lips so sweet,
Nor where the rose and lilies meet;
But a little higher, a little higher,
There, there, O there lies Cupid's fire.

Even in those starry piercing eyes,
There Cupid's sacred fire lies;
Those eyes I strive not to enjoy,
For they have power to destroy:

Nor woo I for a smile or kiss,
So meanly triumphs not my bliss;
But a little higher, a little higher
I climb to crown my chaste desire.

THOMAS CAMPION

185 · PASSING BY

There is a lady sweet and kind,
Was never face so pleased my mind;
I did but see her passing by,
And yet I love her till I die!

Her gestures, motions, and her smile,
Her wit, her voice my heart beguile,
Beguile my heart, I know not why;
And yet I love her till I die!

Cupid is wingèd and doth range
Her country; so my love doth change.
But change the earth or change the sky,
Yet will I love her till I die!

AUTHOR UNKNOWN

I do not love thee for that fair
Rich fan of thy most curious hair;
Though the wires thereof be drawn
Finer than the threads of lawn,
And are softer than the leaves
On which the subtle spider weaves.

I do not love thee for those flowers
Growing on thy cheeks—love's bowers;
Though such cunning them hath spread,
None can paint them white and red:
Love's golden arrows thence are shot,
Yet for them I love thee not.

I do not love thee for those soft
Red coral lips I've kissed so oft;
Nor teeth of pearl, the double guard
To speech whence music still is heard,
Though from those lips a kiss being taken
Might tyrants melt, and death awaken.

I do not love thee, O my fairest,
For that richest, for that rarest
Silver pillar, which stands under
Thy sound head, that globe of wonder;
Though that neck be whiter far
Than towers of polished ivory are.

                                    THOMAS CAREW

187 · I LOVE MY LOVE
IN THE MORNING

I love my love in the morning,
    For she like morn is fair—
Her blushing cheek, its crimson streak,
    It clouds her golden hair.
Her glance, its beam, so soft and kind;
    Her tears, its dewy showers;
And her voice, the tender whispering wind
    That stirs the early bowers.

I love my love in the morning,
    I love my love at noon,
For she is bright as the lord of light,
    Yet mild as autumn's moon:
Her beauty is my bosom's sun,
    Her faith my fostering shade,
And I will love my darling one,
    Till even the sun shall fade.

I love my love in the morning,
    I love my love at even;
Her smile's soft play is like the ray
    That lights the western heaven:
I loved her when the sun was high,
    I loved her when he rose;
But best of all when evening's sigh
    Was murmuring at its close.

GERALD GRIFFIN

188 · SHE WAS A PHANTOM OF DELIGHT

She was a phantom of delight
When first she gleamed upon my sight;
A lovely apparition, sent
To be a moment's ornament;
Her eyes as stars of twilight fair;
Like twilight's, too, her dusky hair;
But all things else about her drawn
From Maytime and the cheerful dawn;
A dancing shape, an image gay,
To haunt, to startle, and waylay.

I saw her upon nearer view,
A spirit, yet a woman too!
Her household motions light and free,
And steps of virgin-liberty;
A countenance in which did meet
Sweet records, promises as sweet;
A creature not too bright or good
For human nature's daily food,
For transient sorrows, simple wiles,
Praise, blame, love, kisses, tears, and smiles.

And now I see with eye serene
The very pulse of the machine;
A being breathing thoughtful breath,
A traveler between life and death;
The reason firm, the temperate will,
Endurance, foresight, strength, and skill;
A perfect woman, nobly planned
To warn, to comfort, and command;
And yet a spirit still, and bright
With something of an angel-light.
                              WILLIAM WORDSWORTH

189 · A VIOLET IN HER HAIR

A violet in her lovely hair,
A rose upon her bosom fair!
    But O, her eyes
A lovelier violet disclose,
And her ripe lips the sweetest rose
    That's 'neath the skies.

A lute beneath her graceful hand
Breathes music forth at her command;
    But still her tongue
Far richer music calls to birth
Than all the minstrel power on earth
    Can give to song.

And thus she moves in tender light,
The purest ray, where all is bright,
    Serene, and sweet;
And sheds a graceful influence round,
That hallows e'en the very ground
    Beneath her feet!

              CHARLES SWAIN

190 · WHITE SHOULDERS

Your white shoulders
    I remember
And your shrug of laughter.

Low laughter
    Shaken slow
From your white shoulders.

              CARL SANDBURG

191 · HE TELLS OF THE PERFECT BEAUTY

O cloud-pale eyelids, dream-dimmed eyes
The poets laboring all their days
To build a perfect beauty in rhyme
Are overthrown by a woman's gaze
And by the unlaboring brood of the skies:
And therefore my heart will bow, when dew
Is dropping sleep, until God burn time,
Before the unlaboring stars and you.

WILLIAM BUTLER YEATS

192 · THE TRIBUTE

No splendor 'neath the sky's proud dome
　　But serves her for familiar wear;
The far-fetched diamond finds its home
　　Flashing and smoldering in her hair;
For her the seas their pearls reveal;
　　Art and strange lands her pomp supply
With purple, chrome, and cochineal,
　　Ocher, and lapis lazuli;
The worm its golden woof presents;
　　Whatever runs, flies, dives, or delves,
All doff for her their ornaments,
　　Which suit her better than themselves;
And all, by this their power to give
　　Proving her right to take, proclaim
Her beauty's clear prerogative
　　To profit so by Eden's blame.

COVENTRY PATMORE

193 · NOCTURNE

All the earth a hush of white,
    White with moonlight all the skies;
Wonder of a winter night—
    And . . . your eyes.

Hues no palette dares to claim
    Where the spoils of sunken ships
Leap to light in singing flame—
    And . . . your lips.

Darkness as the shadows creep
    Where the embers sigh to rest;
Silence of a world asleep—
    And . . . your breast.

AMELIA JOSEPHINE BURR

194 · PASTEL: MASKS AND FACES

The light of our cigarettes
Went and came in the gloom:
It was dark in the little room.

Dark, and then, in the dark,
Sudden, a flash, a glow,
And a hand and a ring I know.

And then, through the dark, a flush
Ruddy and vague, the grace
(A rose!) of her lyric face.

ARTHUR SYMONS

195 · DREAM GIRL

You will come one day in a waver of love,
Tender as dew, impetuous as rain,
The tan of the sun will be on your skin,
The purr of the breeze in your murmuring speech,
You will pose with a hill-flower grace.

You will come, with your slim, expressive arms,
A poise of the head no sculptor has caught
And nuances spoken with shoulder and neck,
Your face in a pass-and-repass of moods
As many as skies in delicate change
Of cloud and blue and flimmering sun.

                    Yet,
You may not come, O girl of a dream,
We may but pass as the world goes by
And take from a look of eyes into eyes,
A film of hope and a memoried day.

CARL SANDBURG

Married

Love

196 · MARRIAGE

Then before all they stand—the holy vow
And ring of gold, no fond illusions now,
Bind her as his. Across the threshold led,
And every tear kissed off as soon as shed,
His house she enters—there to be a light,
Shining within, when all without is night;
A guardian angel o'er his life presiding,
Doubling his pleasures and his cares dividing,
Winning him back when mingling in the throng,
Back from a world we love, alas! too long,
To fireside happiness, to hours of ease,
Blest with that charm, the certainty to please.
How oft her eyes read his; her gentle mind
To all his wishes, all his thoughts inclined;
Still subject—ever on the watch to borrow
Mirth of his mirth and sorrow of his sorrow!
The soul of music slumbers in the shell,
Till waked and kindled by the master's spell,
And feeling hearts—touch them but rightly—pour
A thousand melodies unheard before!

SAMUEL ROGERS

197 · THE POET'S SONG
TO HIS WIFE

How many summers, love,
   Have I been thine?
How many days, thou dove,
   Hast thou been mine?
Time, like the wingèd wind
   When 't bends the flowers,
Hath left no mark behind
   To count the hours!

Some weight of thought, though loth,
   On thee he leaves;
Some lines of care round both
   Perhaps he weaves:
Some fears—a soft regret
   For joys scarce known:
Sweet looks we half forget;
   All else is flown!

Ah! with what thankless heart
   I mourn and sing!
Look where our children start,
   Like sudden spring!
With tongues all sweet and low,
   Like a pleasant rhyme,
They tell how much I owe
   To thee and time!

BARRY CORNWALL

198 · THE WIFE TO HER HUSBAND

Linger not long. Home is not home without thee:
In dearest tokens do but make me mourn.
O, let its memory, like a chain about thee,
Gently compel and hasten thy return!

Linger not long. Though crowds should woo thy
staying,
Bethink thee, can the mirth of thy friend, though
dear,
Compensate for the grief thy long delaying
Costs the fond heart that sighs to have thee here?

Linger not long. How shall I watch thy coming,
As evening shadows stetch o'er moor and dell;
When the wild bee hath ceased her busy humming,
And silence hangs on all things like a spell!

How shall I watch for thee, when fears grow stronger,
As night grows dark and darker on the hill!
How shall I weep, when I can watch no longer!
Ah! art thou absent, art thou absent still?

Yet I shall grieve not, though the eye that seeth me
Gazeth through tears that make its splendor dull;
For oh! I sometimes fear when thou art with me,
My cup of happiness is all too full.

Haste, haste thee home unto thy mountain dwelling,
Haste, as a bird unto its peaceful nest!
Haste, as a skiff, through tempests wide and swelling,
Flies to its haven of securest rest!

Author Unknown

I leaned out of window, I smelt the white clover,
  Dark, dark was the garden, I saw not the gate;
"Now, if there be footsteps, he comes, my one lover—
  Hush, nightingale, hush! O sweet nightingale, wait
        Till I listen and hear
        If a step draweth near,
        For my love he is late!

"The skies in the darkness stoop nearer and nearer,
  A cluster of stars hangs like fruit in the tree,
The fall of the water comes sweeter, comes clearer:
  To what art thou listening, and what dost thou see?
        Let the star-clusters glow,
        Let the sweet waters flow,
        And cross quickly to me.

"You night-moths that hover where honey brims over
  From sycamore blossoms, or settle or sleep;
You glowworms, shine out, and the pathway discover
  To him that comes darkling along the rough steep.
        Ah, my sailor, make haste,
        For the time runs to waste,
        And my love lieth deep—

"Too deep for swift telling; and yet, my one lover,
  I've conned thee an answer, it waits thee tonight."
By the sycamore passed he, and through the white clover;
  Then all the sweet speech I had fashioned took flight;
        But I'll love him more, more
        Than e'er wife loved before,
        Be the days dark or bright.

                      JEAN INGELOW

200 · MY WIFE

Trusty, dusky, vivid, true,
With eyes of gold and bramble-dew,
   Steel-true and blade-straight,
The great artificer
   Made my mate.

Honor, anger, valor, fire;
A love that life could never tire,
   Death quench or evil stir,
The mighty master
   Gave to her.

Teacher, tender, comrade, wife,
A fellow-farer true through life,
   Heart-whole and soul-free
The august father
   Gave to me.
               ROBERT LOUIS STEVENSON

201 · ACROSS THE SKY

Across the sky the daylight crept,
   And birds grew garrulous in the grove,
And on my marriage-morn I slept
   A soft sleep, undisturb'd by love.
               COVENTRY PATMORE

202 · TO MY DEAR AND LOVING HUSBAND

If ever two were one, then surely we;
If ever man were loved by wife, then thee;
If ever wife was happy in a man,
Compare with me, ye women, if you can.
I prize thy love more than whole mines of gold,
Or all the riches that the East doth hold.
My love is such that rivers cannot quench,
Nor aught but love from thee give recompense.
Thy love is such I can no way repay;
The heavens reward thee manifold, I pray.
Then while we live in love let's so persevere
That when we live no more we may live ever.

ANNE BRADSTREET

203 · THE HAPPY HUSBAND

Oft, oft, methinks, the while with thee
   I breathe, as from the heart, thy dear
   And dedicated name, I hear
A promise and a mystery,
   A pledge of more than passing life,
   Yea, in that very name of wife!

A pulse of love that ne'er can sleep!
   A feeling that upbraids the heart
   With happiness beyond desert,
That gladness half requests to weep!
   Nor bless I not the keener sense
   And unalarming turbulence.

Of transient joys, that ask no sting
   From jealous fears, or coy denying;

But born beneath Love's brooding wing,
And into tenderness soon dying,
   Wheel out their giddy moment, then
   Resign the soul to love again;

A more precipitated vein
   Of notes that eddy in the flow
   Of smoothest song, they come, they go,
And leave their sweeter understrain
   Its own sweet self—a love of thee
   That seems, yet cannot greater be!
                    SAMUEL TAYLOR COLERIDGE

204 · THE MARRIAGE RING

The ring, so worn as you behold,
So thin, so pale, is yet of gold:
The passion such it was to prove—
Worn with life's care, love yet was love.
                    GEORGE CRABBE

205 · TO AN ISLE
IN THE WATER

Shy one, shy one,
Shy one of my heart.
She moves in the firelight
Pensively apart.

She carries in the dishes,
And lays them in a row.
To an isle in the water
With her would I go.

She carries in the candles,
And lights the curtained room.
Shy in the doorway
And shy in the gloom;

And shy as a rabbit,
Helpful and shy.
To an isle in the water
With her would I fly.

WILLIAM BUTLER YEATS

206 · MARRIAGE MORNING

Light, so low upon earth,
  You send a flash to the sun.
Here is the golden close of love,
  All my wooing is done.
Oh, the woods and the meadows,
  Woods where we hid from the wet,
Stiles where we stay'd to be kind,
  Meadows in which we met!

Light, so low in the vale,
  You flash and lighten afar,
For this is the golden morning of love,
  And you are his morning star.
Flash, I am coming, I come,
  By meadow and stile and wood,
Oh, lighten into my eyes and heart,
  Into my heart and my blood!

Heart, are you great enough
  For a love that never tires?
O heart, are you great enough for love?
  I have heard of thorns and briers.
Over the thorns and briers,
  Over the meadows and stiles,
Over the world to the end of it
  Flash for a million miles.

ALFRED, LORD TENNYSON

207 · A WEDDING SONG

Two roses growing on a single tree,
Two faces bending o'er a silver spring,
Two pairs of eyes that their own image see,
And set the heavens within a little ring,
Two children in this naughty world of ours,
    Linked by the marriage powers.

Undo the things from off your feet—
This spot at least is holy ground.
The solitude is wild and sweet,
Where no base thing is found.
There watch, or wander in that paradise
    Till soft moonrise.

Sink through the soundless world of dreams,
Or climb the secret stairs of bliss,
And tiptoe stand where brightest gleams
The heaven of heavens within a kiss;
Sleep through the soft hours of rosy morn;
    Urania, be born!

Sleep while the moist star trembles in the dews,
And when in sunrise gleams the lake of glass;
Sleep while the heavens are interchanging hues,
And Saturn's tear "rolls down the blade of glass";
Wake when the birds are singing in the trees,
    And sing like these.

JOHN SAVARY

At length their long kiss severed, with sweet smart:
   And as the last slow sudden drops are shed
   From sparkling eaves when all the storm has fled,
So singly flagged the pulses of each heart.
Their bosoms sundered, with the opening start
   Of married flowers to either side outspread
   From the knit stem; yet still their mouths, burnt
     red,
Fawned on each other where they lay apart.

Sleep sank them lower than the tide of dreams,
   And their dreams watched them sink, and slid away.
Slowly their souls swam up again, through gleams
   Of watered light and dull drowned waifs of day;
Till from some wonder of new woods and streams
   He woke, and wondered more: for there she lay.

DANTE GABRIEL ROSSETTI

As through the land at eve we went,
  And plucked the ripened ears,
We fell out, my wife and I,
  And kissed again with tears.

And blessings on the falling out
  That all the more endears,
When we fall out with those we love
  And kiss again with tears.

For when we came where lies the child
  We lost in other years,
There above the little grave,
O, there above the little grave,
  We kissed again with tears.

                        ALFRED, LORD TENNYSON

The

Anguish

of

Love

210 · LOVE'S PAINS

This love, I canna' bear it,
It cheats me night and day;
This love, I canna' wear it,
It takes my peace away.

This love, wa' once a flower;
But now it is a thorn—
The joy o' evening hour,
Turn'd to a pain e're morn.

This love, it wa' a bud,
And a secret known to me;
Like a flower within a wood;
Like a nest within a tree.

This love, wrong understood,
Oft' turned my joy to pain;
I tried to throw away the bud,
But the blossom would remain.

JOHN CLARE

211 · WHAT CARE I?

Shall I, wasting in despair,
Die because a woman's fair?
Or make pale my cheeks with care
'Cause another's rosy are?
    Be she fairer than the day,
    Or the flowery meads of May;
    If she think not well of me,
    What care I how fair she be?

Shall my silly heart be pined
'Cause I see a woman kind?
Or a well-disposèd nature
Joinèd with a lovely feature?
    Be she meeker, kinder than
    Turtle-dove or pelican;
    If she be not so to me,
    What care I how kind she be?

Shall a woman's virtues move
Me to perish for her love?
Or her well deservings known
Make me quite forget mine own?
    Be she with that goodness blest
    Which may merit name of best;
    If she be not such to me,
    What care I how good she be?

'Cause her fortune seems too high
Shall I play the fool and die?
She that bears a noble mind,
If not outward help she find,
    Thinks what with them he would do
    That without them dares her woo;
    And unless that mind I see,
    What care I how great she be?

Great, or good, or kind, or fair,
I will ne'er the more despair;
If she love me (this believe)
I will die ere she shall grieve.
    If she slight me when I woo,
    I can scorn and let her go;
    For if she be not for me,
    What care I for whom she be?
GEORGE WITHER

212 · SONNET

"Love me, for I love you"—and answer me,
  "Love me, for I love you": so shall we stand
  As happy equals in the flowering land
Of love, that knows not a dividing sea.
Love builds the house on rock and not on sand,
  Love laughs what while the winds rave desperately;
And who hath found love's citadel unmanned?
  And who hath held in bonds love's liberty?
My heart's a coward though my words are brave—
  We meet so seldom, yet we surely part
  So often; there's a problem for your art!
  Still I find comfort in his Book who saith,
Though jealousy be cruel as the grave,
  And death be strong, yet love is strong as death.
CHRISTINA ROSSETTI

213 · COME, REST IN THIS BOSOM

Come, rest in this bosom, my own stricken deer,
Though the herd have fled from thee, thy home is still
    here;
Here still is the smile, that no cloud can o'ercast,
And a heart and a hand all thy own to the last.

Oh! what was love made for, if 'tis not the same
Through joy and through torment, through glory and
    shame?
I know not, I ask not, if guilt's in that heart,
I but know that I love thee, whatever thou art.

Thou hast call'd me thy angel in moments of bliss,
And thy angel I'll be, 'mid the horrors of this—
Through the furnace unshrinking, thy steps to pursue,
And shield thee, and save thee—or perish there too!

                              THOMAS MOORE

214 · YOU SMILED, YOU SPOKE

You smiled, you spoke, and I believed,
By every word and smile deceived.
Another man would hope no more;
Nor hope I what I hoped before:
But let not this last wish be vain;
    Deceive, deceive me once again!
          WALTER SAVAGE LANDOR

215 · THE SUFFERING HEART

No, no, poor suffering heart, no change endeavor;
Choose to sustain the smart, rather than leave her.
My ravished eyes behold such charms about her,
I can die with her, but not live without her.
One tender sigh of hers, to see me languish,
Will more than pay the price of my past anguish.
Beware, O cruel fair, how you smile on me,
'Twas a kind look of yours that has undone me.

Love has in store for me one happy minute,
And she will end my pain who did begin it;
Then, no day void of bliss or pleasure leaving,
Ages shall slide away without perceiving:
Cupid shall guard the door, the more to please us,
And keep out Time and Death, when they would seize
    us:
Time and Death shall depart, and say, in flying,
Love has found out a way to live by dying.

JOHN DRYDEN

Thy strong arms are around me, love,
  My head is on thy breast:
Though words of comfort come from thee,
  My soul is not at rest:

For I am but a startled thing,
  Nor can I ever be
Aught save a bird whose broken wing
  Must fly away from thee.

I cannot give to thee the love
  I gave so long ago—
The love that turned and struck me down
  Amid the blinding snow.

I can but give a sinking heart
  And weary eyes of pain,
A faded mouth that cannot smile
  And may not laugh again.

Yet keep thine arms around me, love,
  Until I drop to sleep:
Then leave me—saying no goodbye,
  Lest I might fall and weep.

ELIZABETH SIDDAL

Stay, O sweet, and do not rise!
The light, that shines, comes from thine eyes.
The day breaks not: it is my heart,
Because that you and I must part.
Stay, or else my joys will die,
And perish in their infancy.

'Tis true, 'tis day: what though it be?
O, wilt thou therefore rise from me?
Why should we rise, because 'tis light?
Did we lie down, because 'twas night?
Love, which in spite of darkness brought us hither,
Should in despite of light keep us together.

Light hath no tongue, but is all eye.
If it could speak as well as spy,
This were the worst that it could say:
That, being well, I fain would stay,
And that I lov'd my heart and honor so,
That I would not from her, that had them, go.

Must business thee from hence remove?
O, that's the worst disease of love!
The poor, the foul, the false, love can,
Admit, but not the busied man.
He, which hath business, and makes love, doth do
Such wrong, as when a married man doth woo.

JOHN DONNE

If you but knew
How all my days seemed filled with dreams of you,
How sometimes in the silent night
Your eyes thrill through me with their tender light,
How oft I hear your voice when others speak,
How you 'mid other forms I seek—
Oh, love more real than though such dreams were
    true,
If you but knew.

Could you but guess
How you alone make all my happiness,
How I am more than willing for your sake
To stand alone, give all and nothing take,
Nor chafe to think you bound while I am free,
Quite free, till death, to love you silently,
Could you but guess.

Could you but learn
How when you doubt my truth I sadly yearn
To tell you all, to stand for one brief space
Unfettered, soul to soul, as face to face,
To crown you king, my king, till life shall end,
My lover and likewise my truest friend,
Would you love me, dearest, as fondly in return,
Could you but learn?

AUTHOR UNKNOWN

219 · THE LYRIC

The wandering airs they faint
On the dark, the silent stream—
The champak odors fail
Like sweet thoughts in a dream;
The nightingale's complaint,
It dies upon her heart;
As I must on thine,
Oh, belovèd as thou art!

Oh lift me from the grass!
I die! I faint! I fail!
Let thy love in kisses rain
On my lips and eyelids pale.
My cheek is cold and white, alas!
My heart beats loud and fast;
Oh! press it to thine own again,
Where it will break at last.

Percy Bysshe Shelley

220 · LOVE AND THE ROSE

The rose is fairest when 'tis budding new,
   And hope is brightest when it dawns from fears:
The rose is sweetest washed with morning dew,
   And love is loveliest when embalmed in tears.
O wilding rose, whom fancy thus endears,
   I bid your blossoms in my bonnet wave,
Emblem of hope and love through future years!

Sir Walter Scott

Before I trust my fate to thee,
  Or place my hand in thine,
Before I let thy future give
  Color and form to mine,
Before I peril all for thee,
Question thy soul tonight for me.

I break all slighter bonds, nor feel
  A shadow of regret:
Is there one link within the past
  That holds thy spirit yet?
Or is thy faith as clear and free
As that which I can pledge to thee?

Does there within thy dimmest dreams
  A possible future shine,
Wherein thy life could henceforth breathe,
  Untouched, unshared by mine?
If so, at any pain or cost,
O, tell me before all is lost!

Look deeper still: if thou canst feel,
  Within thy inmost soul,
That thou hast kept a portion back,
  While I have staked the whole,
Let no false pity spare the blow,
But in true mercy tell me so.

Is there within thy heart a need
  That mine cannot fulfill?
One chord that any other hand
  Could better wake or still?
Speak now, lest at some future day
My whole life wither and decay.

Lives there within thy nature hid
   The demon-spirit, change,
Shedding a passing glory still
   On all things new and strange?
It may not be thy fault alone—
But shield my heart against thine own.

Couldst thou withdraw thy hand one day
   And answer to my claim,
That fate, and that today's mistake—
   Not thou—had been to blame?
Some soothe their conscience thus; but thou
Wilt surely warn and save me now.

Nay, answer *not*—I dare not hear,
   The words would come too late;
Yet I would spare thee all remorse,
   So comfort thee, my fate:
Whatever on my heart may fall,
Remember, I *would* risk it all!

ADELAIDE ANNE PROCTER

222 · APRIL IS IN MY MISTRESS' FACE

April is in my mistress' face,
And July in her eyes hath place,
Within her bosom is September,
But in her heart a cold December.

AUTHOR UNKNOWN

Escape me?
Never—
Beloved!
While I am I, and you are you,
So long as the world contains us both,
Me the loving and you the loth,
While the one eludes, must the other pursue.
My life is a fault at last, I fear:
It seems too much like a fate, indeed!
Though I do my best I shall scarce succeed.

But what if I fail of my purpose here?
It is but to keep the nerves at strain,
To dry one's eyes and laugh at a fall,
And, baffled, get up to begin again—
So the chase takes up one's life, that's all.
While, look but once from your farthest bound
At me so deep in the dust and dark,
No sooner the old hope drops to ground
Than a new one, straight to the selfsame mark,
I shape me—
Ever
Removed!

ROBERT BROWNING

224 · OBLATION

Ask nothing more of me, sweet;
   All I can give you I give;
   Heart of my heart, were it more,
More should be laid at your feet:
   Love that should help you to live—
   Song that should spur you to soar.

All things were nothing to give,
   Once to have sense of you more—
   Touch you and taste of you, sweet,
Think you and breathe you, and live
   Swept of your wings as they soar,
   Trodden by chance of your feet.

I, who have love and no more,
   Bring you but love of you, sweet.
   He that hath more, let him give;
He that hath wings, let him soar:
   Mine is the heart at your feet
   Here, that must love you to live.
                ALGERNON CHARLES SWINBURNE

225 · LOVE IS A SECRET
FEEDING FIRE

Love is a secret feeding fire that gives all creatures
    being,
Life to the dead, speech to the dumb, and to the blind
    man seeing.
And yet in me he contradicts all these his sacred
    graces:
Sears up my lips, my eyes, my life, and from me ever
    flying
Leads me in paths untracked, ungone, and many
    uncouth places,
Where in despair I beauty curse. Curse love and all
    fair faces!

AUTHOR UNKNOWN

226 · THE PRIMROSE

Ask me why I send you here
This sweet infanta of the year?
   Ask me why I send to you
This primrose, thus bepearled with dew?
   I will whisper to your ears,
The sweets of love are mixed with tears.

   Ask me why this flower does show
So yellow-green, and sickly too?
   Ask me why the stalk is weak
And bending (yet it doth not break?),
   I will answer: These discover
What fainting hopes are in a lover.

ROBERT HERRICK

227 · SONNET

At whiles (yea oftentimes) I muse over
   The quality of anguish that is mine
   Through Love: then pity makes my voice to pine
Saying, "Is any else thus, anywhere?"
Love smiteth me, whose strength is ill to bear;
   So that of all my life is left no sign
   Except one thought; and that, because 'tis thine,
Leaves not the body but abideth there.
And then if I, whom other aid forsook,
   Would aid myself, and innocent of art
     Would fain have sight of thee as a last hope,
No sooner do I lift mine eyes to look
   Than the blood seems as shaken from my heart,
     And all my pulses beat at once and stop.

DANTE ALIGHIERI
translated by Dante Gabriel Rossetti

228 · THE PITY OF LOVE

A pity beyond all telling
Is hid in the heart of love:
The folk who are buying and selling;
The clouds on their journey above;
The cold wet winds ever blowing;
And the shadowy hazel grove
Where mouse-gray waters are flowing
Threaten the head that I love.

WILLIAM BUTLER YEATS

Let's contend no more, love,
   Strive nor weep:
All be as before, love,
   —only sleep!

What's so wild as words are?
   I and thou
In debate, as birds are,
   Hawk on bough!

See the creatures stalking
   While we speak!
Hush and hide the talking,
   Cheek on cheek!

What so false as truth is,
   False to thee?
Where the serpent's tooth is,
   Shun the tree—

Where the apple reddens
   Never pry—
Lest we lose our Edens,
   Eve and I!

Be a god and hold me
   With a charm!
Be a man and fold me
   With thine arm!

Teach me, only teach love!
   As I ought.
I will speak thy speech, love,
   Think thy thought—

Meet, if thou require it,
   Both demands,
Laying flesh and spirit
   In thy hands.

That shall be tomorrow,
   Not tonight:
I must bury sorrow
   Out of sight:

—Must a little weep, love,
   (foolish me!)
And so fall asleep, love,
   Loved by thee.
                    ROBERT BROWNING

230 · THE LOVER COMPARETH HIS STATE TO A SHIP IN PERILOUS STORM TOSSED ON THE SEA

My galley charged with forgetfulness,
Through sharp seas in winter nights doth pass
'Tween rock and rock, and eke mine enemy, alas,
That is my lord, steereth with cruelness,
And every oar a thought in readiness,
As though that death were light in such a case.
An endless wind doth tear the sail apace,
Of forced sighs and trusty fearfulness.
A rain of tears, a cloud of dark disdain,
Hath done the weared cords great hinderance;
Wreathed with error and eke with ignorance.
The stars be hid that led me to this pain;
Drowned is reason that should me comfort,
And I remain despairing of the port.
                    SIR THOMAS WYATT

231 · SONG

Absent from thee, I languish still;
   Then ask me not, when I return?
The straying fool 'twill plainly kill
   To wish all day, all night to mourn.

Dear! from thine arms then let me fly,
   That my fantastic mind may prove
The torments it deserves to try
   That tears my fixed heart from my love.

When, wearied with a world of woe,
   To thy safe bosom I retire
Where love and peace and truth does flow,
   May I contented there expire,

Lest, once more wandering from that heaven,
   I fall on some base heart unblessed,
Faithless to thee, false, unforgiven,
   And lose my everlasting rest.

John Wilmot

232 · IT IS THE SEASON OF THE SWEET WILD ROSE

It is the season of the sweet wild rose,
My lady's emblem in the heart of me!
So golden-crowned shines she gloriously,
And with that softest dream of blood she glows:
Mild as an evening heaven round Hesper bright!
I pluck the flower, and smell it, and revive
The time when in her eyes I stood alive.
I seem to look upon it out of night.

Here's madam, stepping hastily. Her whims
Bid her demand the flower, which I let drop.
As I proceed, I feel her sharply stop,
And crush it under heel with trembling limbs.
She joins me in a catlike way, and talks
Of company, and even condescends
To utter laughing scandal of old friends.
These are the summer days, and these our walks.

GEORGE MEREDITH

233 · SONNET

Loving in truth, and fain in verse my love to show,
That she, dear she, might take some pleasure of my pain:
Pleasure might cause her read, reading might make her know,
Knowledge might pity win, and pity grace obtain,
   I sought fit words to paint the blackest face of woe,
Studying inventions fine, her wits to entertain:
Oft turning others' leaves to see if thence would flow
Some fresh and fruitful showers upon my sun-burn'd brain.
   But words came halting forth, wanting Invention's stay,
Invention, Nature's child, fled step-dame Study's blows,
And others' feet still seem'd but strangers in my way.
Thus great with child to speak, and helpless in my throes,
   Biting my trewand pen, beating myself for spite,
   Fool, said my Muse to me, look in thy heart and write.

SIR PHILIP SIDNEY

234 · HE BIDS HIS BELOVED
BE AT PEACE

I hear the Shadowy Horses, their long manes a-shake,
Their hoofs heavy with tumult, their eyes glimmering
    white;
The North unfolds above them clinging, creeping
    night,
The East her hidden joy before the morning break,
The West weeps in pale dew and sighs passing away,
The South is pouring down roses of crimson fire:
O vanity of Sleep, Hope, Dream, endless Desire,
The Horses of Disaster plunge in the heavy clay:
Beloved, let your eyes half close, and your heart beat
Over my heart, and your hair fall over my breast,
Drowning love's lonely hour in deep twilight of rest,
And hiding their tossing manes and their tumultuous
    feet.

                        WILLIAM BUTLER YEATS

235 · BEHOLD, LOVE, THY POWER

Behold, Love, thy power how she despiseth!
My great pain how little she regardeth!
　　The holy oath, whereof she taketh no cure,
　　Broken she hath; and yet she bideth sure
Right at her ease and little she dreadeth.
Weaponed thou art, and she unarmed sitteth;
To the disdainful her life she leadeth,
　　To me spiteful without cause or measure,
　　Behold, Love.

I am in hold: if pity thee moveth,
Go bend thy bow, that stony hearts breaketh,
　　And with some stroke revenge the displeasure
　　Of thee and him, that sorrow doth endure,
And, as his lord, the lowly entreateth.
　　Behold, Love.

SIR THOMAS WYATT

My love is of a birth as rare
As 'tis for object strange and high:
It was begotten by Despair
Upon Impossibility.

Magnanimous Despair alone
Could show me so divine a thing,
Where feeble Hope could ne'er have flown
But vainly flapped its tinsel wing.

And yet I quickly might arrive
Where my extended soul is fixt,
But Fate does iron wedges drive,
And always crowds itself betwixt.

For Fate with jealous eye does see
Two perfect loves; nor lets them close:
Their union would her ruin be,
And her tyrannic power depose.

And therefore her decrees of steel
Us as the distant poles have placed,
(Though love's whole world on us doth wheel)
Not by themselves to be embraced.

Unless the giddy heaven fall,
And earth some new convulsion tear;
And, us to join, the world should all
Be cramped into a planisphere.

As lines so loves oblique may well
Themselves in every angle greet:
But ours so truly parallel,
Though infinite, can never meet.

Therefore the love which us doth bind
But Fate so enviously debars,
Is the conjunction of the mind,
And opposition of the stars.

ANDREW MARVELL

237 · HE WISHES HIS BELOVED
WERE DEAD

Were you but lying cold and dead,
And lights were paling out of the West,
You would come hither, and bend your head,
And I would lay my head on your breast;
And you would murmur tender words,
Forgiving me, because you were dead:
Nor would you rise and hasten away,
Though you have the will of the wild birds,
But know your hair was bound and wound
About the stars and moon and sun:
O would beloved that you lay
Under the dock-leaves in the ground,
While lights were paling one by one.

WILLIAM BUTLER YEATS

238 · AH! YESTERDAY WAS DARK AND DREAR

Ah! yesterday was dark and drear,
  My heart was deadly sore;
Without thy love it seemed, my dear,
  That I could live no more.

And yet I laugh and sing today;
  Care or care not for me,
Thou canst not take the love away
  With which I worship thee.

And if tomorrow, dear, I live,
  My heart I shall not break:
For still I hold it that to give
  Is sweeter than to take.

MATHILDE BLIND

"And how could you dream of meeting?"
   Nay, how can you ask me, sweet?
All day my pulse had been beating
   The tune of your coming feet.

And as nearer and ever nearer
   I felt the throb of your tread,
To be in the world grew dearer,
   And my blood ran rosier red.

Love called, and I could not linger,
   But sought the forbidden tryst,
As music follows the finger
   Of the dreaming lutanist.

And though you had said it and said it,
   "We must not be happy today,"
Was I not wiser to credit
   The fire in my feet than your nay?

              JAMES RUSSELL LOWELL

240 · SURRENDER

As I look back upon your first embrace
I understand why from your sudden touch
Angered I sprang, and struck you in the face.
You asked at once too little and too much.
But now that of my spirit you require
Love's very soul that unto death endures,
Crown as you will the cup of your desire—
    I am all yours.

AMELIA JOSEPHINE BURR

241 · THE SORROW OF LOVE

The quarrel of the sparrows in the eaves,
The full round moon and the star-laden sky,
And the loud song of the ever-singing leaves,
Had hid away earth's old and weary cry.

And then you came with those red mournful lips,
And with you came the whole of the world's tears,
And all the trouble of her laboring ships,
And all the trouble of her myriad years.

And now the sparrows warring in the eaves,
The curd-pale moon, the white stars in the sky,
And the loud chaunting of the unquiet leaves,
Are shaken with earth's old and weary cry.

WILLIAM BUTLER YEATS

When passion's trance is overpast,
If tenderness and truth could last,
Or live, whilst all wild feelings keep
Some mortal slumber, dark and deep,
I should not weep, I should not weep!

It were enough to feel, to see,
Thy soft eyes gazing tenderly,
And dream the rest—and burn and be
The secret food of fires unseen,
Couldst thou but be as thou hast been.

After the slumber of the year
The woodland violets reappear;
All things revive in field or grove,
And sky and sea, but two, which move
And form all others—life, and love.

PERCY BYSSHE SHELLEY

243 · THE LONELY ROAD

Here, ever since you went abroad,
  If there be change, no change I see;
I only walk our wonted road,
  The road is only walkt by me.

Yes; I forgot; a change there is;
  Was it of *that* you bade me tell?
I catch at times, at times I miss
  The sight, the tone, I know so well.

Only two months since you stood here!
  Two shortest months! then tell me why
Voices are harsher than they were,
  And tears are longer ere they dry.

WALTER SAVAGE LANDOR

244 · RENOUNCEMENT

I must not think of thee; and, tired yet strong,
I shun the thought that lurks in all delight—
The thought of thee—and in the blue heaven's height,
And in the dearest passage of a song.
Oh, just beyond the fairest thoughts that throng
This breast, the thought of thee waits, hidden yet bright
But it must never, never come in sight;
I must stop short of thee the whole day long.
But when sleep comes to close each difficult day,
When night gives pause to the long watch I keep,
And all my bonds I needs must loose apart,
Must doff my will as raiment laid away—
With the first dream that comes with the first sleep
I run, I run, I am gathered to thy heart.

ALICE MEYNELL

245 · RED AND WHITE ROSES

Read in these roses the sad story
Of my hard fate, and your own glory.
  In the white you may discover
  The paleness of a fainting lover;
In the red the flames still feeding
On my heart, with fresh wounds bleeding.
  The white will tell you how I languish,
  And the red express my anguish;
The white my innocence displaying,
The red my martyrdom betraying.
  The frowns that on your brow resided,
  Have those roses thus divided.
Oh! let your smiles but clear the weather,
And then they both shall grow together.

THOMAS CAREW

246 · THE PLEA

Kind in unkindness, when will you relent
And cease with faint love true love to torment?
Still entertained, excluded still I stand,
Her glove still hold, but cannot touch her hand.

In her fair hand my hopes and comforts rest:
O might my fortunes with that hand be blest!
No envious breaths then my deserts could shake
For they are good whom such true love doth make.

O let not beauty so forget her birth
That it should fruitless home return to earth!
Love is the fruit of beauty, then love one—
Not your sweet self, for such self-love is none.

Love one that only lives in loving you,
Whose wronged deserts would you with pity view.
This strange distaste which your affection sways
Would relish love, and you find better days.

Thus till my happy sight your beauty views,
Whose sweet remembrance still my hope renews,
Let these poor lines solicit love for me
And place my joys where my desires would be.

THOMAS CAMPION

I envy seas whereon he rides,
   I envy spokes of wheels
Of chariots that him convey,
   I envy speechless hills

That gaze upon his journey;
   How easy all can see
What is forbidden utterly
   As heaven, unto me!

I envy nests of sparrows
   That dot his distant eaves,
The wealthy fly upon his pane,
   The happy, happy leaves

That just abroad his window
   Have summer's leave to be,
The earrings of Pizarro
   Could not obtain for me.

I envy light that wakes him,
   And bells that boldly ring
To tell him it is noon abroad—
   Myself his noon could bring,

Yet interdict my blossom
   And abrogate my bee,
Lest noon in everlasting night
   Drop Gabriel and me.
              EMILY DICKINSON

248 · IN THREE DAYS

So, I shall see her in three days
And just one night, but nights are short,
Then two long hours, and that is morn.
See how I come, unchanged, unworn!
Feel, where my life broke off from thine,
How fresh the splinters keep and fine—
Only a touch and we combine!

Too long, this time of year, the days!
But nights, at least the nights are short.
As night shows where her one moon is,
A hand's-breadth of pure light and bliss,
So life's night gives my lady birth
And my eyes hold her! What is worth
The rest of heaven, the rest of earth?

O loaded curls, release your store
Of warmth and scent, as once before
The tingling hair did, lights and darks
Outbreaking into fairy sparks,
When under curl and curl I pried
After the warmth and scent inside,
Thro' lights and darks how manifold—
The dark inspired, the light controlled!
As early Art embrowns the gold.

What great fear, should one say, "Three days
"That change the world might change as well
"Your fortune; and if joy delays,
"Be happy that no worse befell!"
What small fear, if another says,
"Three days and one short night beside
"May throw no shadow on your ways;

—212—

"But years must teem with change untried,
"With chance not easily defied,
"With an end somewhere undescried."
No fear!—or if a fear be born
This minute, it dies out in scorn.
Fear? I shall see her in three days
And one night, now the nights are short,
Then just two hours, and that is morn.

ROBERT BROWNING

249 · LOVE IN ABSENCE

Like as the culver on the bared bough
Sits mourning for the absence of her mate,
And in her songs sends many a wishful vow
For his return, that seems to linger late;
So I alone, now left disconsolate,
Mourn to myself the absence of my love,
And wandering here and there all desolate,
Seek with my plaints to match that mournful dove.
No joy of ought that under heaven doth hove
Can comfort me, but her own joyous sight,
Whose sweet aspect both god and man can move,
In her unspotted pleasance to delight:
Dark is my day whiles her fair light I miss,
And dead my life, that wants such lively bliss.

EDMUND SPENSER

250 · COME, O COME

Come, O come, my life's delight,
   Let me not in languor pine!
Love loves no delay; thy sight,
   The more enjoyed, the more divine:
O come, and take from me
The pain of being deprived of thee!

Thou all sweetness dost enclose,
   Like a little world of bliss.
Beauty guards thy looks: the rose
   In them pure and eternal is.
Come, then, and make thy flight
As swift to me, as heavenly light.

THOMAS CAMPION

251 · WHEN I WOULD IMAGE

When I would image her features,
   Comes up a shrouded head:
I touch the outlines, shrinking;
   She seems of the wandering dead.

But when love asks for nothing,
   And lies on his bed of snow,
The face slips under my eyelids,
   All in its living glow.

Like a dark cathedral city,
   Whose spires, and domes, and towers
Quiver in violet lightnings,
   My soul basks on for hours.

GEORGE MEREDITH

252 · TO FANNY

I cry your mercy—pity—love!—aye, love!—
  Merciful love that tantalizes not,
One-thoughted, never-wandering, guileless love,
  Unmasked, and being seen—without a blot!
O! let me have thee whole—all—all—be mine!
  That shape, that fairness, that sweet minor zest
Of love, your kiss—those hands, those eyes divine,
  That warm, white, lucent, million-pleasured breast—
Yourself—your soul—in pity give me all,
  Withhold no atom's atom or I die,
Or living on perhaps, your wretched thrall,
  Forget, in the midst of idle misery,
  Life's purposes—the palate of my mind
Losing its gust, and my ambition blind!

JOHN KEATS

253 · SONG

I wish I was where I would be
With love alone to dwell;
Was I but her or she but me
Then love would all be well.

I wish to send my thoughts to her
As quick as thoughts can fly;
But as the winds the waters stir
The mirrors change and fly.

JOHN CLARE

254 · WE MUST NOT PART

We must not part, as others do,
With sighs and tears as we were two;
Though with these outward forms we part,
We keep each other in our heart.
What search hath found a being, where
I am not, if that thou be there?

True love hath wings, and can as soon
Survey the world, as sun and moon;
And everywhere our triumphs keep
O'er absence, which makes others weep;
By which alone a power is given
To live on earth, as they in heaven.

AUTHOR UNKNOWN

255 · A WOMAN'S PRIDE

I will not look for him, I will not hear
My heart's loud beating, as I strain to see
Across the rain forlorn and hopelessly,
Nor, starting, think 'tis he that draws so near.
I will forget how tenderly and dear
He might in coming hold his arms to me,
For I will prove what woman's pride can be
When faint love lingers in the darkness drear.
I will not—ah, but should he come tonight
I think my life might break through very bliss,
This little will should so be torn apart
That all my soul might fail in golden light
And let me die; so do I long for this.
Ah, love, thine eyes!—Nay, love—Thy heart, thy heart!

HELEN HAY

256 · LONGING

Come to me in my dreams, and then
By day I shall be well again!
For then the night will more than pay
The hopeless longing of the day.

Come, as thou cam'st a thousand times,
A messenger from radiant climes,
And smile on thy new world, and be
As kind to others as to me!

Or, as thou never cam'st in sooth,
Come now, and let me dream it truth;
And part my hair, and kiss my brow,
And say: *My love! why sufferest thou?*

Come to me in my dreams, and then
By day I shall be well again!
For then the night will more than pay
The hopeless longing of the day.

MATTHEW ARNOLD

257 · YOU AND I

My hand is lonely for your clasping, dear;
  My ear is tired waiting for your call.
I want your strength to help, your laugh to cheer;
  Heart, soul and senses need you, one and all.
I droop without your full, frank sympathy;
  We ought to be together—you and I;
We want each other so, to comprehend
    The dream, the hope, things planned, or seen,
      or wrought.
Companion, comforter and guide and friend,
  As much as love asks love, does thought ask thought.
Life is so short, so fast the lone hours fly,
  We ought to be together, you and I.

Henry Alford

258 · FORGIVEN

I dreamed so dear a dream of you last night!
I thought you came. I was so glad, so gay,
I whispered, "Those were foolish words to say;
I meant them not. I cannot bear the sight
Of your dear face. I cannot meet the light
Of your dear eyes upon me. Sit, I pray—
Sit here beside me; turn your look away,
And lay your cheek on mine." Till morning bright
We sat so, and we did not speak. I knew
All was forgiven; so I nestled there
With your arms round. Swift the sweet hours flew.
At last I waked, and sought you everywhere.
How long, dear, think you, that my glad cheek will
Burn—as it burns with your cheek's pressure still?

Helen Hunt Jackson

259 · OF HIS LADY
AMONG OTHER LADIES

With other women I beheld my love;
  Not that the rest were women to mine eyes,
Who only as her shadows seem'd to move.

I do not praise her more than with the truth,
  Nor blame I these if it be rightly read.

But while I speak, a thought I may not soothe
  Says to my senses: "Soon shall ye be dead,
  If for my sake your tears ye will not shed."

And then the eyes yield passage, at that thought,
To the heart's weeping, which forgets her not.

GUIDO CAVALCANTI
translated by Dante Gabriel Rossetti

260 · SONG

I walk'd in the lonesome evening,
   And who so sad as I,
When I saw the young men and maidens
   Merrily passing by.
      To thee, my Love, to thee—
      So fain would I come to thee!
While the ripples fold upon sands of gold
   And I look across the sea.

I stretch out my hands; who will clasp them?
   I call—thou repliest no word:
O why should heart-longing be weaker
   Than the waving wings of a bird!
      To thee, my Love, to thee—
      So fain would I come to thee!
For the tide's at rest from east to west,
   And I look across the sea.

There's joy in the hopeful morning,
   There's peace in the parting day,
There's sorrow with every lover
   Whose true love is far away.
      To thee, my Love, to thee—
      So fain would I come to thee!
And the water's bright in a still moonlight,
   As I look across the sea.

WILLIAM ALLINGHAM

261 · IF

If I had but two little wings,
   And were a little feathery bird,
      To you I'd fly, my dear!
But thoughts like these are idle things,
      And I stay here.

But in my sleep to you I fly;
   I'm always with you in my sleep,
      The world is all one's own.
But then one wakes, and where am I?
      All, all alone.

Sleep stays not, though a monarch bids;
   So I love to wake ere break of day:
      For though my sleep be gone,
Yet while 'tis dark, one shuts one's lids,
      And still dreams on.
                    SAMUEL TAYLOR COLERIDGE

262 · WESTERN WIND

Western wind, when wilt thou blow,
The small rain down can rain?
Christ, that my love were in my arms,
And I in my bed again.
                    AUTHOR UNKNOWN

263 · AT THE CHURCH GATE

Although I enter not,
Yet round about the spot
   Ofttimes I hover:
And near the sacred gate,
With longing eyes I wait,
   Expectant of her.

The minster bell tolls out
Above the city's rout
   And noise and humming
They've hushed the minster bell:
The organ 'gins to swell:
   She's coming, she's coming!

My lady comes at last,
Timid, and stepping fast,
   And hastening hither,
With modest eyes downcast:
She comes—she's here—she's past—
   May heaven go with her!

Kneel, undisturb'd, fair saint!
Pour out your praise or plaint
   Meekly and duly;
I will not enter there,
To sully your pure prayer
   With thoughts unruly.

But suffer me to pace
Round the forbidden place,
   Lingering a minute,
Like outcast spirits who wait
And see through heaven's gate
   Angels within it.
       WILLIAM MAKEPEACE THACKERAY

264 · THE NYMPH'S REPLY
TO THE SHEPHERD

If all the world and love were young,
And truth in every shepherd's tongue,
These pretty pleasures might me move
To live with thee and be thy love.

But Time drives flocks from field to fold;
When rivers rage and rocks grow cold;
And Philomel becometh dumb;
The rest complains of cares to come.

The flowers do fade, and wanton fields
To wayward Winter reckoning yields:
A honey tongue, a heart of gall,
Is fancy's spring, but sorrow's fall.

Thy gowns, thy shoes, thy beds of roses,
Thy cap, thy kirtle, and thy posies,
Soon break, soon wither—soon forgotten,
In folly ripe, in reason rotten.

Thy belt of straw and ivy-buds,
Thy coral clasps and amber studs—
All these in me no means can move
To come to thee and be thy love.

But could youth last, and love still breed,
Had joys no date, nor age no need,
Then these delights my mind might move
To live with thee and be thy love.

SIR WALTER RALEIGH

265 · TO ———

One word is too often profaned
    For me to profane it,
One feeling too falsely disdained
    For thee to disdain it;
One hope is too like despair
    For prudence to smother,
And pity from thee more dear
    Than that from another.

I can give not what men call love,
    But wilt thou accept not
The worship the heart lifts above
    And the heavens reject not—
The desire of the moth for the star,
    Of the night for the morrow,
The devotion to something afar
    From the sphere of our sorrow?
              PERCY BYSSHE SHELLEY

266 · LOVE'S WISDOM

How long I've loved thee, and how well—
    I dare not tell!
Because, if thou shouldst once divine
    This love of mine,
Or did but once my tongue confess
    My heart's distress,
Far, far too plainly thou wouldst see
    My slavery,
And, guessing what Love's wit should hide,
    Rest satisfied!

So, though I worship at thy feet,
    I'll be discreet—
And all my love shall not be told,
    Lest thou be cold,
And, knowing I was always thine,
    Scorn to be mine.
So am I dumb, to rescue thee
    From tyranny—
And, by my silence, I do prove
    wisdom and love!

MARGARET DELAND

267 · SHE SCHOOLS THE FLIGHTY PUPILS OF HER EYES

She schools the flighty pupils of her eyes,
With levell'd lashes stilling their disquiet;
She puts in leash her pair'd lips lest surprise
Bare the condition of a realm at riot.
If he suspect that she has ought to sigh at
His injury she'll avenge with raging shame.
She kept her love-thoughts on most lenten diet,
And learnt her not to startle at his name.

GERARD MANLEY HOPKINS

I hid my love when young while I
Couldn't bear the buzzing of a fly;
I hid my love to my despite
Till I could not bear to look at light.
I dare not gaze upon her face
But left her memory in each place,
Where ere I saw a wildflower lie
I kissed and bade my love goodbye.

I met her in the greenest dells
Where dewdrops pearl the wood bluebells;
The lost breeze kissed her bright blue eye
The bee kissed and went singing by.
A sunbeam found a passage there,
A gold chain round her neck so fair;
As secret as the wild bee's song,
She lay there all the summer long.

I hid my love in field and town
Till e'en the breeze would knock me down;
The bees seemed singing ballads o'er
The fly's buzz turned a lion's roar.
And even silence found a tongue
To haunt me all the summer long;
The riddle nature could not prove
Was nothing else but secret love.

JOHN CLARE

269 · NEVER THE TIME
AND THE PLACE

Never the time and the place
   And the loved one all together!
This path—how soft to pace!
   This May—what magic weather!
Where is the loved one's face?
In a dream that loved one's face meets mine,
   But the house is narrow, the place is bleak
Where, outside, rain and wind combine
   With a furtive ear, if I strive to speak,
   With hostile eye at my flushing cheek,
With a malice that marks each word, each sign!
O enemy sly and serpentine
   Uncoil thee from the waking man!
      Do I hold the past
      Thus firm and fast
   Yet doubt if the future hold I can
This path so soft to pace shall lead,
Thro' the magic of May to herself indeed!
Or narrow if needs the house must be,
Outside are the storms and strangers: we—
Oh, close, safe, warm sleep I and she,
—I and she!

Robert Browning

I cannot live with you,
It would be life,
And life is over there
Behind the shelf

The sexton keeps the key to,
Putting up
Our life, his porcelain,
Like a cup

Discarded of the housewife,
Quaint or broken;
A newer Sèvres pleases,
Old ones crack.

I could not die with you,
For one must wait
To shut the other's gaze down—
You could not.

And I, could I stand by
And see you freeze,
Without my right of frost,
Death's privilege?

Nor could I rise with you,
Because your face
Would put out Jesus',
That new grace

Glow plain and foreign
On my homesick eye,
Except that you, than he
Shone closer by.

They'd judge us—how?
For you served heaven, you know,
Or sought to;
I could not,

Because you saturated sight,
And I had no more eyes
For sordid excellence
As paradise.

And were you lost, I would be,
Though my name
Rang loudest
On the heavenly fame.

And were you saved,
And I condemned to be
Where you were not,
That self were hell to me.

So we must keep apart,
You there, I here,
With just the door ajar
That oceans are,
And prayer,
And that pale sustenance,
Despair!

EMILY DICKINSON

271 · SONNET

Fair is my love that feeds among the lilies,
  The lilies growing in the pleasant garden,
Where Cupid's mount, that well-beloved hill is,
  And where that little god himself is warden.
See where my love sits in the beds of spices,
  Beset all round with camphor, myrrh, and roses,
And interlac'd with curious devices,
  Which her from all the world apart incloses.
There doth she tune her lute for her delight,
  And with sweet music makes the ground to move,
Whilst I (poor I) do sit in heavy plight,
  Wailing alone my unrespected love,
Not daring to rush into so rare a place,
That gives to her, and she to it, a grace.

Bartholomew Griffin

272 · TOO LATE

Each on his own strict line we move,
And some find death ere they find love.
So far apart their lives are thrown
From the twin soul that halves their own.

And sometimes, by still harder fate,
The lovers meet, but meet too late.
—Thy heart is mine!—*True, true! ah, true!*
Then, love, thy hand!—*Ah, no! adieu!*

Matthew Arnold

273 · SONNET

How like a winter hath my absence been
From thee, the pleasure of the fleeting year!
What freezings have I felt, what dark days seen!
What old December's bareness everywhere!
And yet this time removed was summer's time;
The teeming autumn, big with rich increase,
Bearing the wanton burthen of the prime,
Like widowed wombs after their lords' decease:
Yet this abundant issue seem'd to me
But hope of orphans and unfather'd fruit;
For summer and his pleasures wait on thee,
And, thou away, the very birds are mute;
    Or, if they sing 'tis with so dull a cheer
    That leaves look pale, dreading the winter's near.

WILLIAM SHAKESPEARE

274 · SONNET

From you have I been absent in the spring,
When proud-pied April, dress'd in all his trim,
Hath put a spirit of youth in everything,
That heavy Saturn laugh'd and leap'd with him.
Yet nor the lays of birds, nor the sweet smell
Of different flowers in odor and in hue,
Could make me any summer's story tell,
Or from their proud lap pluck them where they grew:
Nor did I wonder at the lily's white,
Nor praise the deep vermilion in the rose;
They were but sweet, but figures of delight,
Drawn after you, you pattern of all those.
    Yet seem'd it winter still, and, you away,
    As with your shadow I with these did play.

WILLIAM SHAKESPEARE

275 · SONNET

Those lips that Love's own hand did make
Breathed forth the sound that said "I hate,"
To me that languish'd for her sake.
But when she saw my woeful state,
Straight in her heart did mercy come,
Chiding that tongue that ever sweet
Was used in giving gentle doom;
And taught it thus anew to greet;
"I hate" she alter'd with an end,
That follow'd it as gentle day
Doth follow night, who, like a fiend,
From heaven to hell is flown away;
    "I hate" from hate away she threw,
    And saved my life, saying "not you."
WILLIAM SHAKESPEARE

276 · SONNET

Unlike are we, unlike, O princely heart!
Unlike our uses and our destinies.
Our ministering two angels look surprise
On one another, as they strike athwart
Their wings in passing. Thou, bethink thee, art
A guest for queens to social pageantries,
With gages from a hundred brighter eyes
Than tears even can make mine, to play thy part
Of chief musician. What hast *thou* to do
With looking from the lattice-lights at me,
A poor, tired, wandering singer . . . singing through
The dark, and leaning up a cypress tree?
The chrism is on thine head—on mine, the dew—
And Death must dig the level where these agree.
ELIZABETH BARRETT BROWNING

277 · SONNET

And wilt thou have me fashion into speech
The love I bear thee, finding words enough,
And hold the torch out, while the winds are rough
Between our faces, to cast light on each?
I drop it at thy feet. I cannot teach
My hand to hold my spirit so far off
From myself . . . me . . . that I should bring thee proof
In words, of love hid in me out of reach.
Nay, let the silence of my womanhood
Commend my woman-love to thy belief—
Seeing that I stand unwon, however wooed,
And rend the garment of my life, in brief,
By a most dauntless, voiceless fortitude,
Lest one touch of this heart convey its grief.

ELIZABETH BARRETT BROWNING

278 · SONNET

If I leave all for thee, wilt thou exchange
And be all to me? Shall I never miss
Home-talk and blessing and the common kiss
That comes to each in turn, nor count it strange,
When I look up, to drop on a new range
Of walls and floors . . . another home than this?
Nay, wilt thou fill that place by me which is
Filled by dead eyes too tender to know change?
That's hardest. If to conquer love, has tried,
To conquer grief, tries more . . . as all things prove,
For grief indeed is love and grief beside.
Alas, I have grieved so I am hard to love.
Yet love me—wilt thou? Open thine heart wide,
And fold within, the wet wings of thy dove.

ELIZABETH BARRETT BROWNING

279 · TO HIS COY LOVE

I pray thee love, love me no more,
   Call home the heart you gave me,
I but in vain that saint adore,
   That can, but will not save me:
These poor half kisses kill me quite;
   Was ever man thus served?
Amidst an ocean of delight,
   For pleasure to be starved.

Show me no more those snowy breasts,
   With azure rivers branched,
Where whilst my eye with plenty feasts,
   Yet is my thirst not stanched.
O Tantalus, thy pains ne'er tell,
   By me thou art prevented;
'Tis nothing to be plagu'd in hell,
   But thus in heaven tormented.

Clip me no more in those dear arms,
   Nor thy life's comfort call me;
O, these are but too powerful charms,
   And do but more enthrall me.
But see how patient I am grown,
   In all this coyle about thee;
Come, nice thing, let thy heart alone.
   I cannot live without thee.

MICHAEL DRAYTON

280 · SONG

Why so pale and wan, fond lover?
    Prithee, why so pale?
Will, when looking well can't move her,
    Looking ill prevail?
    Prithee, why so pale?

Why so dull and mute, young sinner?
    Prithee, why so mute?
Will, when speaking well can't win her,
    Saying nothing do't?
    Prithee, why so mute?

Quit, quit for shame! This will not move;
    This cannot take her.
If of herself she will not love,
    Nothing can make her:
    The devil take her.

                          SIR JOHN SUCKLING

281 · THOU HAST NOT RAIS'D, IANTHE, SUCH DESIRE

Thou hast not rais'd, Ianthe, such desire
    In any breast as thou hast rais'd in mine.
No wandering meteor now, no marshy fire,
    Leads on my steps, but lofty, but divine:

And, if thou chillest me, as chill thou dost
    When I approach too near, too boldly gaze,
So chills the blushing morn, so chills the host
    Of vernal stars, with light more chaste than day's.

                       WALTER SAVAGE LANDOR

282 · THE APPARITION

When by thy scorn, O murd'ress, I am dead,
   And that thou thinkst thee free
From all solicitation from me,
Then shall my ghost come to thy bed,
And thee, fain'd vestal, in worse arms shall see;
Then thy sick taper will begin to wink,
And he, whose thou art then, being tir'd before,
Will, if thou stir, or pinch to wake him, think
   Thou call'st for more,
And in false sleep will from thee shrink,
And then poor aspen wretch, neglected thou
Bath'd in a cold quicksilver sweat wilt lie
A verier ghost than I;
What I will say, I will not tell thee now,
Lest that preserve thee; and since my love is spent,
I had rather thou shouldst painfully repent,
Than by my threat'nings rest still innocent.

John Donne

283 · SWEET, LET ME GO

Sweet, sweet, sweet, let me go,
What do you mean, to vex me so,
Cease, cease, cease your pleading force,
Do you think thus, to extort remorse,
Now, now, now no more. Alas you overbear me,
And I would cry, but some would hear, I fear me.

Author Unknown

284 · NON SUM QUALIS ERAM BONAE SUB REGNO CYNARAE

Last night, ah, yesternight, betwixt her lips and mine
There fell thy shadow, Cynara! Thy breath was shed
Upon my soul between the kisses and the wine;
And I was desolate and sick of an old passion—
Yea, I was desolate and bowed my head.
I have been faithful to thee, Cynara!—In my fashion.

All night upon mine heart I felt her warm heart beat,
Night-long within mine arms in love and sleep she lay;
Surely the kisses of her bought red mouth were sweet;
But I was desolate and sick of an old passion,
When I woke and found the dawn was gray:
I have been faithful to thee, Cynara!—In my fashion.

I have forgot much, Cynara! Gone with the wind,
Flung roses, roses riotously with the throng,
Dancing, to put thy pale, lost lilies out of mind;
But I was desolate and sick of an old passion—
Yea, all the time, because the dance was long:
I have been faithful to thee, Cynara!—In my fashion.

I cried for madder music and for stronger wine,
But when the feast is finished and the lamps expire,
Then falls thy shadow, Cynara! The night is thine;
And I am desolate and sick of an old passion,
Yea, hungry for the lips of my desire:
I have been faithful to thee, Cynara!—In my fashion.

ERNEST DOWSON

I loved thee once, I'll love no more,
  Thine be the grief as is the blame;
Thou art not what thou wast before,
  What reason I should be the same?
    He that can love unloved again,
    Hath better store of love than brain:
  God send me love my debts to pay,
  While unthrifts fool their love away.

Nothing could have my love o'erthrown,
  If thou hadst still continued mine;
Yea, if thou hadst remained thy own,
  I might perchance have yet been thine.
    But thou thy freedom did recall,
    That if thou might elsewhere inthrall;
  And then how could I but disdain
  A captive's captive to remain?

When new desires had conquered thee,
  And changed the object of thy will,
It had been lethargy in me,
  Not constancy, to love thee still.
    Yea, it had been a sin to go
    And prostitute affection so,
  Since we are taught no prayers to say
  To such as must to others pray.

Yet do thou glory in thy choice,
  Thy choice of his good fortune boast;
I'll neither grieve nor yet rejoice,
  To see him gain what I have lost;
    The height of my disdain shall be,
    To laugh at him, to blush for thee;
  To love thee still, but go no more
  A begging to a beggar's door.

                  SIR ROBERT AYTON

I do confess thou'rt smooth and fair,
  And I might have gone near to love thee,
Had I not found the slightest prayer
  That lips could move, had power to move thee;
But I can let thee now alone
As worthy to be loved by none.

I do confess thou'rt sweet; yet find
  Thee such an unthrift of thy sweets,
Thy favors are but like the wind
  That kisseth everything it meets:
And since thou canst with more than one,
Thou'rt worthy to be kissed by none.

The morning rose that untouched stands
  Armed with her briers, how sweet she smells!
But plucked and strained through ruder hands,
  Her sweets no longer with her dwells:
But scent and beauty both are gone,
And leaves fall from her, one by one.

Such fate ere long will thee betide
  When thou hast handled been awhile,
With sere flowers to be thrown aside;
  And I shall sigh, while some will smile,
To see thy love to every one
Hath brought thee to be loved by none.

Sir Robert Ayton

287 · SONG: TO MY INCONSTANT MISTRESS

When thou, poor excommunicate
　　From all the joys of love, shalt see
The full reward and glorious fate
　　Which my strong faith shall purchase me,
　　Then curse thine own inconstancy.

A fairer hand than thine shall cure
　　That heart, which thy false oaths did wound;
And to my soul a soul more pure
　　Than thine shall by Love's hand be bound,
　　And both with equal glory crown'd.

Then shalt thou weep, entreat, complain
　　To Love, as I did once to thee;
When all thy tears shall be as vain
　　As mine were then, for thou shalt be
　　Damn'd for thy false apostasy.

THOMAS CAREW

288 · SONNET

Dear, why make you more of a dog than me?
  If he do love, I burn, I burn in love:
  If he wait well, I never thence would move:
If he be fair, yet but a dog can be.
Little he is, so little worth is he;
  He barks, my songs thine own voice oft doth prove:
  Bidd'n, perhaps he fetcheth thee a glove,
But I unbid, fetch even my soul to thee.
  Yet while I languish, him that bosom clips,
That lap doth lap, nay lets, in spite of spite,
This sour-breath'd mate taste of those sugar'd lips.
Alas, if you grant only such delight
  To witless things, then love I hope (since wit
  Becomes a clog) will soon ease me of it.

Sir Philip Sidney

289 · WHEN I LOVED YOU

When I loved you, I can't but allow
  I had many an exquisite minute;
But the scorn that I feel for you now
  Hath even more luxury in it!

Thus, whether we're on or we're off,
  Some witchery seems to await you;
To love you is pleasant enough,
  But oh! 'tis delicious to hate you!

Thomas Moore

My lute awake! perform the last
Labor that thou and I shall waste,
And end that I have now begun;
For when this song is sung and past,
My lute be still, for I have done.

As to be heard where ear is none,
As lead to grave in marble stone,
My song may pierce her heart as soon;
Should we then sigh, or sing, or moan?
No, no, my lute, for I have done.

The rocks do not so cruelly
Repulse the waves continually,
As she my suit and affection,
So that I am past remedy:
Whereby my lute and I have done.

Proud of the spoil that thou hast got
Of simple hearts thorough love's shot,
By whom, unkind, thou hast them won,
Think not he hath his bow forgot,
Although my lute and I have done.

Vengeance shall fall on thy disdain,
That makest but game on earnest pain;
Think not alone under the sun
Unquit to cause thy lovers plain,
Although my lute and I have done.

Perchance thee lie withered and old,
The winter nights that are so cold,
Plaining in vain unto the moon;

Thy wishes then dare not be told;
Care then who list, for I have done.

And then may chance thee to repent
The time that thou hast lost and spent
To cause thy lovers sigh and swoon;
Then shalt thou know beauty but lent,
And wish and want as I have done.

Now cease, my lute! this is the last
Labor that thou and I shall waste,
And ended is that we begun;
Now is this song both sung and past:
My lute, be still, for I have done.

SIR THOMAS WYATT

291 · NO SECOND TROY

Why should I blame her that she filled my days
With misery, or that she would of late
Have taught to ignorant men most violent ways,
Or hurled the little streets upon the great,
Had they but courage equal to desire?
What could have made her peaceful with a mind
That nobleness made simple as a fire,
With beauty like a tightened bow, a kind
That is not natural in an age like this,
Being high and solitary and most stern?
Why, what could she have done being what she is?
Was there another Troy for her to burn?

WILLIAM BUTLER YEATS

292 · SINCE FIRST I SAW YOUR FACE

Since first I saw your face I resolved to honor and reknown
    ye;
If now I am disdainèd I wish my heart had never known ye.
What? I that loved and you that liked, shall we begin to
    wrangle?
No, no, no, my heart is fast, and cannot disentangle.
If I admire or praise you too much, that fault you may forgive
    me;
Or if my hands had stray'd but a touch, then justly might
    you leave me.
I ask'd you leave, you bade me love; is't now a time to chide
    me?
No, no, no, I'll love you still what fortune e'er betide me.
The Sun, whose beams most glorious are, rejecteth no
    beholder,
And your sweet beauty past compare made my poor eyes the
    bolder.
Where beauty moves and wit delights and signs of kindness
    bind me,
There, O there, whe'er I go I'll leave my heart behind me!

Author Unknown

293 · SONG: MEDIOCRITY IN LOVE
REJECTED

Give me more love or more disdain;
    The torrid or the frozen zone
Bring equal ease unto my pain,
    The temperate affords me none:
Either extreme of love or hate,
Is sweeter than a calm estate.

Give me a storm; if it be love,
  Like Danaë in that golden shower,
I swim in pleasure; if it prove
  Disdain, that torrent will devour
My vulture-hopes; and he's possess'd
Of heaven, that's but from hell released.
    Then crown my joys or cure my pain:
    Give me more love or more disdain.

                                    THOMAS CAREW

294 · MY LOVE IS LIKE TO ICE

My love is like to ice, and I to fire:
How comes it then that this her cold so great
Is not dissolved through my so hot desire,
But harder grows the more I her entreat?
Or how comes it that my exceeding heat
Is not allayed by her heart-frozen cold,
But that I burn much more in boiling sweat,
And feel my flames augmented manifold?
What more miraculous thing may be told,
That fire, which all things melts, should harden ice,
And ice, which is congeal'd with senseless cold,
Should kindle fire by wonderful device?
Such is the power of love in gentle mind,
That it can alter all the course of kind.

                                    EDMUND SPENSER

295 · THOSE EYES

Ah! do not wanton with those eyes,
  Lest I be sick with seeing;
Nor cast them down, but let them rise,
  Lest shame destroy their being.

Ah! be not angry with those fires,
  For then their threats will kill me;
Nor look too kind on my desires,
  For then my hopes will spill me.

Ah! do not steep them in thy tears,
  For so will sorrow slay me;
Nor spread them as distraught with fears—
  Mine own enough betray me.

                              BEN JONSON

296 · WHEN FIRST I MET THEE

When first I met thee, warm and young,
  There shone such truth about thee,
And on thy lip such promise hung,
  I did not dare to doubt thee,
I saw thee change, yet still relied,
  Still clung with hope the fonder,
And thought, though false to all beside,
  From me thou couldst not wander.
        But go, deceiver! go—
          The heart, whose hopes could make it
        Trust one so false, so low,
          Deserves that thou shouldst break it.

When every tongue thy follies named,
  I fled the unwelcome story;

Or found, in even the faults they blamed,
   Some gleams of future glory.
I still was true, when nearer friends
   Conspired to wrong, to slight thee;
The heart, that now thy falsehood rends,
   Would then have bled to right thee.
        But go, deceiver! go—
          Some day, perhaps, thou'lt waken
        From pleasure's dream, to know
          The grief of hearts forsaken.

Even now, though youth its bloom has shed,
   No lights of age adorn thee:
The few who loved thee once have fled,
   And they who flatter scorn thee.
Thy midnight cup is pledged to slaves,
   No genial ties enwreathe it;
The smiling there, like light on graves,
   Has rank cold hearts beneath it.
        Go—go—though worlds were thine
          I would not now surrender
        One taintless tear of mine
          For all thy guilty splendor!

And days may come, thou false one! yet,
   When even those ties shall sever;
When thou wilt call, with vain regret,
   On her thou'st lost forever;
On her who, in thy fortune's fall,
   With smiles hath still received thee,
And gladly died to prove thee all
   Her fancy first believed thee.
        Go—go—'tis vain to curse,
         'Tis weakness to upbraid thee;
        Hate cannot wish thee worse
         Than guilt and shame have made thee.
                  THOMAS MOORE

297 · SONG

See, see, she wakes, Sabina wakes!
  And now the sun begins to rise;
Less glorious is the morn that breaks
  From his bright beams than her fair eyes.

With light united, day they give,
  But different fates ere night fulfill.
How many by his warmth will live!
  How many will her coldness kill!

WILLIAM CONGREVE

298 · PHYLLIS

Phyllis is my only joy,
  Faithless as the winds or seas,
Sometimes coming, sometimes coy,
  Yet she never fails to please:
    If with a frown
    I am cast down,
    Phyllis smiling
    And beguiling
Makes me happier than before.

Though, alas! too late I find
  Nothing can her fancy fix,
Yet the moment she is kind
  I forgive her all her tricks,
    Which though I see
    I can't get free.
    She deceiving,
    I believing,
What need lovers wish for more?

SIR CHARLES SEDLEY

The
Twilight
of
Love

299 · WILL YOU LOVE ME
WHEN I'M OLD?

I would ask of you, my darling,
  A question soft and low,
That gives me many a heartache
  As the moments come and go.

Your love I know is truthful,
  But the truest love grows cold;
It is this that I would ask you:
  Will you love me when I'm old?

Life's morn will soon be waning,
  And its evening bells be tolled,
But my heart shall know no sadness,
  If you'll love me when I'm old.

Down the stream of life together
  We are sailing side by side,
Hoping some bright day to anchor
  Safe beyond the surging tide.
Today our sky is cloudless,
  But the night may clouds unfold;
But, though storms may gather round us,
  Will you love me when I'm old?

When my hair shall shade the snowdrift,
  And mine eyes shall dimmer grow,
I would lean upon some loved one,
  Through the valley as I go.
I would claim of you a promise,
  Worth to me a world of gold;
It is only this, my darling,
  That you'll love me when I'm old.

AUTHOR UNKNOWN

300 · OH, NO—NOT EV'N WHEN FIRST WE LOV'D

Oh, no—not ev'n when first we lov'd
   Wert thou as dear as now thou art;
Thy beauty then my senses mov'd,
   But now thy virtues bind my heart.
What was but Passion's sigh before
   Has since been turn'd to Reason's vow;
And, though I then might love thee *more*,
   Trust me, I love thee *better* now.

Although my heart in earlier youth
   Might kindle with more wild desire,
Believe me, it has gain'd in truth
   Much more than it has lost in fire.
The flame now warms my inmost core
   That then but sparkled o'er my brow,
And though I seem'd to love thee more,
   Yet, oh, I love thee better now.

THOMAS MOORE

301 · I HAVE NEVER LOVED YOU YET

I have never loved you yet, if now I love.

If Love was born in that bright April sky
And ran unheeding when the sun was high,
And slept as the moon sleeps through Autumn nights
While those clear steady stars burn in their heights:

If Love so lived and ran and slept and woke
And ran in beauty when each morning broke,
Love yet was boylike; fervid and unstable,
Teased with romance, not knowing truth from fable.

But Winter after Autumn comes and stills
The petulant waters and the wild mind fills
With silence; and the dark and cold are bitter,
O, bitter to remember past days sweeter.

Then Spring with one warm cloudy finger breaks
The frost and the heart's airless black soil shakes;
Love grown a man uprises, serious, bright
With mind remembering now things dark and light.

O, if young Love was beautiful, Love grown old,
Experienced and grave is not grown cold.
Life's faithful fire in Love's heart burns the clearer
With all that was, is and draws darkling nearer.

I have never loved you yet, if now I love.

JOHN FREEMAN

302 · TO CHLOE, WHO FOR HIS SAKE
WISHED HERSELF YOUNGER

There are two births; the one when light
   First strikes the new awaken'd sense;
The other when two souls unite,
   And we must count our life from thence:
When you loved me and I loved you
The both of us were born anew.

Love then to us new souls did give
   And in those souls did plant new powers;
Since when another life we live,
   The breath we breathe is his, not ours:
Love makes those young whom age doth chill,
And whom he finds young keeps young still.

WILLIAM CARTWRIGHT

Yes, still I love thee! Time, who sets
   His signet on my brow,
And dims my sunken eye, forgets
   The heart he could not bow,
Where love, that cannot perish, grows
For one, alas! that little knows
   How love may sometimes last,
Like sunshine wasting in the skies,
   When clouds are overcast.

The dewdrop hanging o'er the rose,
   Within its robe of light,
Can never touch a leaf that blows,
   Though seeming to the sight;
And yet it still will linger there,
Like hopeless love without despair—
   A snowdrop in the sun:
A moment finely exquisite,
   Alas! but only one.

I would not have thy married heart
   Think momently of me;
Nor would I tear the cords apart,
   That bind me so to thee;
No! while my thoughts seem pure and mild,
Like dew upon the roses wild,
   I would not have thee know
The stream, that seems to thee so still,
   Has such a tide below.

Enough that in delicious dreams
   I see thee and forget—
Enough, that when the morning beams
   I feel my eyelids wet!

Yet, could I hope, when Time lets fall
The darkness for creation's pall,
    To meet thee—and to love—
I would not shrink from aught below,
    Nor ask for more above.
                              RUFUS DAWES

304 · NOT OURS THE VOWS

Not ours the vows of such as plight
    Their troth in sunny weather,
While leaves are green, and skies are bright,
    To walk on flowers together.

But we have loved as those who tread
    The thorny path of sorrow,
With clouds above, and cause to dread
    Yet deeper gloom tomorrow.

That thorny path, those stormy skies,
    Have drawn our spirits nearer;
And rendered us, by sorrow's ties,
    Each to the other dearer.

Love, born in hours of joy and mirth,
    With mirth and joy may perish;
That to which darker hours gave birth
    Still more and more we cherish.

It looks beyond the clouds of time,
    And through death's shadowy portal;
Made by adversity sublime,
    By faith and hope immortal.
                              BERNARD BARTON

305 · WHEN SHE COMES HOME

When she comes home again! A thousand ways
I fashion, to myself, the tenderness
Of my glad welcome: I shall tremble—yes;
And touch her, as when first in the old days
I touched her girlish hand, nor dared upraise
Mine eyes, such was my faint heart's sweet distress.
Then silence: and the perfume of her dress:
The room will sway a little, and a haze
Cloy eyesight—soulsight, even—for a space;
And tears—yes; and the ache here in the throat,
To know that I so ill deserve the place
Her arms make for me; and the sobbing note
I stay with kisses, ere the tearful face
Again is hidden in the old embrace.

JAMES WHITCOMB RILEY

306 · WE HAVE LIVED AND
LOVED TOGETHER

We have lived and loved together
   Through many changing years;
We have shared each other's gladness
   And wept each other's tears;
I have known ne'er a sorrow
   That was long unsoothed by thee;
For thy smiles can make a summer
   Where darkness else would be.

Like the leaves that fall around us
   In autumn's fading hours,

Are the traitor's smiles, that darken
  When the cloud of sorrow lowers;
And though many such we've known, love,
  Too prone, alas, to range,
We both can speak of one love
  Which time can never change.

We have lived and loved together
  Through many changing years,
We have shared each other's gladness
  And wept each other's tears.
And let us hope the future,
  As the past has been will be:
I will share with thee my sorrows,
  And thou thy joys with me.

CHARLES JEFFERYS

307 · TO A LADY, ON HER ART OF GROWING OLD GRACEFULLY

You ask a verse, to sing (ah, laughing face!)
Your happy art of growing old with grace?
O Muse, begin, and let the truth—but hold!
First let me see that you are growing old.

JOHN JAMES PIATT

I played with you 'mid cowslips blowing,
When I was six and you were four;
When garlands weaving, flower-balls throwing,
Were pleasures soon to please no more.
Through groves and meads, o'er grass and heather,
With little playmates, to and fro,
We wandered hand in hand together—
But that was sixty years ago.

You grew a lovely roseate maiden,
And still our early love was strong;
Still with no care our days were laden,
They glided joyously along;
And I did love you, very dearly,
How dearly words want power to show;
I thought your heart was touched as nearly—
But that was fifty years ago.

Then other lovers came around you,
Your beauty grew from year to year,
And many a splendid circle found you
The center of its glittering sphere.
I saw you then, first vows forsaking,
On rank and wealth your hand bestow;
Oh, then I thought my heart was breaking—
But that was forty years ago.

And I lived on, to wed another:
No cause she gave me to repine;
And when I heard you were a mother,
I did not wish the children mine.
My own young flock, in fair progression,
Made up a pleasant Christmas row:
My joy in them was past expression—
But that was thirty years ago.

You grew a matron plump and comely,
You dwelt in fashion's brightest blaze;
My earthly lot was far more homely;
But I too had my festal days.
No merrier eyes have ever glistened
Around the hearthstone's wintry glow,
Than when my youngest child was christened—
But that was twenty years ago.

Time passed. My eldest girl was married,
And I am now a grandsire gray;
One pet of four years old I've carried
Among the wild-flowered meads to play.
In our old fields of childish pleasure,
Where now, as then, the cowslips blow,
She fills her basket's ample measure—
And that is not ten years ago.

But though first love's impassioned blindness
Has passed away in colder light,
I still have thought of you with kindness,
And shall do, till our last goodnight.
The ever-rolling silent hours
Will bring a time we shall not know,
When our young days of gathering flowers
Will be a hundred years ago.

THOMAS LOVE PEACOCK

309 · WHEN YOU ARE OLD

When you are old and gray and full of sleep,
And nodding by the fire, take down this book,
And slowly read, and dream of the soft look
Your eyes had once, and of their shadows deep;

How many loved your moments of glad grace,
And loved your beauty with love false or true;
But one man loved the pilgrim soul in you,
And loved the sorrows of your changing face.

And bending down beside the glowing bars
Murmur, a little sadly, how love fled
And paced upon the mountains overhead
And hid his face amid a crowd of stars.

WILLIAM BUTLER YEATS

310 · SONNET

That time of year thou mayst in me behold
When yellow leaves, or none, or few, do hang
Upon those boughs which shake against the cold,
Bare ruin'd choirs, where late the sweet birds sang.
In one thou see'st the twilight of such day
As after sunset fadeth in the west;
Which by and by black night doth take away,
Death's second self, that seals up all in rest.
In me thou see'st the glowing of such fire,
That on the ashes of his youth doth lie,
As the death-bed whereon it must expire,
Consumed with that which it was nourish'd by.
    This thou perceivest, which makes thy love more
        strong,
    To love that well which thou must leave ere long.

WILLIAM SHAKESPEARE

Farewell, love, and all thy laws forever:
Thy baited hooks shall tangle me no more;
Senec and Plato call me from thy lore,
To perfect wealth my wit for to endeavor.
In blind error when I did persever,
Thy sharp repulse, that pricketh ay so sore,
Hath taught me to set in trifles no store,
And scape forth, since liberty is lever.
Therefore, farewell: go trouble younger hearts,
And in me claim no more authority;
With idle youth go use thy property,
And thereon spend thy many brittle darts;
For hitherto though I have lost all my time,
Me lusteth no longer rotten boughs to climb.

Sir Thomas Wyatt

O the years I lost before I knew you,
    Love!
O, the hills I climbed and came not to you,
    Love!
Ah! who shall render unto us to make
    Us glad,
The things which for and of each other's sake
    We might have had?

If you and I had sat and played together,
    Love,
Two speechless babes in the summer weather,
    Love,
By one sweet brook which, though it dried up long
    Ago,
Still makes for me today a sweeter song
    Than all I know—

If hand-in-hand through the mysterious gateway,
    Love,
Of womanhood, we had first looked and straightway,
    Love,
Had whispered to each other softly, ere
    It yet
Was dawn, what now in noonday heat and fear
    We both forget—

If all of this had given its completeness,
    Love,
To every hour, would it be added sweetness,
    Love?
Could I know sooner whether it were well
    Or ill
With thee? One wish could I more sweetly tell,
    More swift fulfill?

Ah! vainly thus I sit and dream and ponder,
      Love,
Losing the precious present while I wonder,
      Love,
About the days in which you grew and came
      To be
So beautiful, and did not know the name
      Or sight of me.

But all lost things are in the angels' keeping,
      Love;
No past is dead for us, but only sleeping,
      Love;
The years of heaven will all earth's little pain
      Make good,
Together there we can begin again,
      In babyhood.

HELEN HUNT JACKSON

313 · LOVE AND AGE

Loves flies with bow unstrung when Time appears,
And trembles at the approach of heavy years.
A few bright feathers leaves he in his flight,
Quite beyond recall, but not forgotten quite.

WALTER SAVAGE LANDOR

314 · THE CHESSBOARD

My little love, do you remember,
  Ere we were grown so sadly wise,
Those evenings in the bleak December,
Curtained warm from the snowy weather,
When you and I played chess together,
  Checkmated by each other's eyes?

Ah! still I see your soft white hand
Hovering warm o'er queen and knight;
  Brave pawns in valiant battle stand;
The double castles guard the wings;
The bishop, bent on distant things,
Moves, sidling, through the fight.

Our fingers touch; our glances meet,
And falter; falls your golden hair
  Against my cheek; your bosom sweet
Is heaving. Down the field, your queen
Rides slow, her soldiery all between,
  And checks me unaware.

Ah me! the little battle's done:
Disperst is all its chivalry.
Full many a move since then have we
Mid life's perplexing checkers made,
And many a game with fortune played;
  What is it we have won?
  This, this at least—if this alone:

That never, never, nevermore,
As in those old still nights of yore,
  (Ere we were grown so sadly wise,)
  Can you and I shut out the skies,
Shut out the world and wintry weather,
  And, eyes exchanging warmth with eyes,
Play chess, as then we played together.
ROBERT BULWER, LORD LYTTON

Lost

Love

315 · ONE FOND KISS
AND THEN WE SEVER

One fond kiss, and then we sever!
One farewell, and then forever!
Deep in heart-wrung tears I'll pledge thee,
Warring sighs and groans I'll wage thee.

Who shall say that Fortune grieves him,
While the star of Hope she leaves him?
Me, no cheerful twinkle lights me;
Dark despair around benights me.

I'll ne'er blame my partial fancy,
Nothing could resist my Nancy:
But to see her was to love her;
Love but her, and love forever.

Had we never loved so kindly,
Had we never loved so blindly,
Never met or never parted,
We had ne'er been broken-hearted.

Fare thee well, thou first and fairest!
Fare thee well, thou best and dearest!
Thine be every joy and treasure,
Peace, enjoyment, love, and pleasure!

One fond kiss, and then we sever!
One farewell, alas, for ever!
Deep in heart-wrung tears I'll pledge thee,
Warring sighs and groans I'll wage thee.

ROBERT BURNS

316 · HEART, WE WILL FORGET HIM

Heart, we will forget him!
  You and I, tonight!
You may forget the warmth he gave,
  I will forget the light.

When you have done, pray tell me,
  That I my thoughts may dim;
Haste! lest while you're lagging,
  I may remember him!
                    EMILY DICKINSON

317 · ON PARTING

The kiss, dear maid! thy lip has left
  Shall never part from mine,
Till happier hours restore the gift
  Untainted back to thine.

Thy parting glance, which fondly beams,
  An equal love may see;
The tear that from thine eyelid streams
  Can weep no change in me.

I ask no pledge to make me blest
  In gazing when alone;
Nor one memorial for a breast,
  Whose thoughts are all thine own.

Nor need I write—to tell the tale
  My pen were doubly weak:
Oh! what can idle words avail,
  Unless the heart could speak?

By day or night, in weal or woe,
  That heart, no longer free,
Must bear the love it cannot show,
  And silent ache for thee.
    GEORGE GORDON, LORD BYRON

318 · SONNET

Since there's no help, come, let us kiss and part,
Nay, I have done: you get no more of me,
And I am glad, yea glad with all my heart,
That thus so cleanly, I myself can free.
Shake hands forever, cancel all our vows,
And, when we meet at any time again,
Be it not seen in either of our brows
That we one jot of former love retain.
Now at the last gasp of Love's latest breath,
When, his pulse failing, passion speechless lies,
When Faith is kneeling by his bed of death,
And Innocence is closing up his eyes,
  Now if thou wouldst, when all have given him over,
  From death to life, thou might'st him yet recover.
    MICHAEL DRAYTON

We were apart; yet, day by day,
I bade my heart more constant be.
I bade it keep the world away,
And grow a home for only thee;
Nor feared but thy love likewise grew,
Like mine, each day, more tried, more true.

The fault was grave! I might have known,
What far too soon, alas! I learned—
The heart can bind itself alone,
And faith may oft be unreturned.
Self-swayed our feelings ebb and swell—
Thou lov'st no more—Farewell! Farewell!

Farewell!—and thou, thou lonely heart,
Which never yet without remorse
Even for a moment didst depart
From thy remote and spherèd course
To haunt the place where passions reign—
Back to thy solitude again!

Back! with the conscious thrill of shame
Which Luna felt, that summer night,
Flash through her pure immortal frame,
When she forsook the starry height
To hang over Endymion's sleep
Upon the pine-grown Latmian steep.

Yet she, chaste queen, had never proved
How vain a thing is mortal love,
Wandering in heaven, far removed.
But thou hast long had place to prove
This truth—to prove, and make thine own:
"Thou has been, shalt be, art, alone."

Or, if not quite alone, yet they
Which touch thee are unmating things—
Ocean and clouds and night and day;
Lorn autumns and triumphant springs;
And life, and others' joy and pain,
And love, if love, of happier men.

MATTHEW ARNOLD

320 · APRIL LOVE

We have walked in Love's land a little way,
  We have learnt his lesson a little while,
And shall we not part at the end of day,
    With a sigh, a smile?

A little while in the shine of the sun,
  We were twined together, joined lips forgot
How the shadows fall when the day is done,
    And when Love is not.

We have made no vows—there will none be broke,
  Our love was free as the wind on the hill,
There was no word said we need wish unspoke,
    We have wrought no ill.

So shall we not part at the end of day,
  Who have loved and lingered a little while,
Join lips for the last time, go our way,
    With a sigh, a smile.

ERNEST DOWSON

321 · SONNET

When last I roved these winding wood walks green;
Green winding walks, and shady pathways sweet,
Oft-times would Anna seek the silent scene,
Shrouding her beauties in the lone retreat.
No more I hear her footsteps in the shade;
Her image only in these pleasant ways
Meets me self-wandering, where, in happier days,
I held free converse with the fair-hair'd maid.
I pass'd the little cottage which she loved,
The cottage which did once my all contain;
It spake of days which ne'er must come again;
Spake to my heart, and much my heart was moved.
"Now fair befall thee, gentle maid!" said I
And from the cottage turn'd me with a sigh.

CHARLES LAMB

322 · THE LOST MISTRESS

All's over, then: does truth sound bitter
    As one at first believes?
Hark, 'tis the sparrows' goodnight twitter
    About your cottage eaves!

And the leaf-buds on the vine are woolly,
    I noticed that, today;
One day more bursts them open fully
    —You know the red turns gray.

Tomorrow we meet the same then, dearest?
    May I take your hand in mine?
Mere friends are we—well, friends the merest
    Keep much that I'll resign:

For each glance of that eye so bright and black,
  Though I keep with heart's endeavor—
Your voice, when you wish the snowdrops back,
  Though it stay in my soul forever!

Yet I will but say what mere friends say,
  Or only a thought stronger;
I will hold your hand but as long as all may,
  Or so very little longer!

                              ROBERT BROWNING

323 · THE GARLAND I SEND THEE

The garland I send thee was culled from those bowers
Where thou and I wandered in long vanished hours;
Not a leaf or a blossom its bloom here displays,
But bears some remembrance of those happy days.

The roses were gathered by that garden gate,
Where our meetings, though early, seemed always too
    late;
Where ling'ring full oft through a summer-night's
    moon,
Our partings, though late, appeared always too soon.

The rest were all culled from the banks of that glade,
Where, watching the sunset, so often we strayed,
And mourned, as the time went, that Love had no
    power
To bind in his chain even one happy hour.

                              THOMAS MOORE

We parted in silence, we parted by night,
  On the banks of that lonely river;
Where the fragrant limes their boughs unite,
  We met—and we parted forever!
The night-bird sung, and the stars above
  Told many a touching story,
Of friends long passed to the kingdom of love,
  Where the soul wears its mantle of glory.

We parted in silence—our cheeks were wet
  With the tears that were past controlling;
We vowed we would never—no, never forget,
  And those vows at the time were consoling;
But those lips that echoed the wounds of mine
  Are as cold as that lonely river;
And that eye, that beautiful spirit's shrine,
  Has shrouded its fires forever.

And now on the midnight sky I look,
  And my heart grows full of weeping;
Each star is to me a sealed book,
  Some tale of that loved one keeping.
We parted in silence—we parted in tears,
  On the banks of that lonely river:
But the color and bloom of those bygone years
  Shall hang o'er its waters forever.

                                        MRS. CRAWFORD

325 · ECHO

Come to me in the silence of the night;
  Come in the speaking silence of a dream;
Come with soft rounded cheeks and eyes as bright
    As sunlight on a stream;
    Come back in tears;
O memory, hope, love of finished years.

O dream how sweet, too sweet, too bittersweet,
  Whose wakening should have been in paradise,
Where souls brimful of love abide and meet;
    Where thirsting longing eyes
    Watch the slow door
That, opening, letting in, lets out no more.

Yet come to me in dreams, that I may live
  My very life again though cold in death:
Come back to me in dreams, that I may give
    Pulse for pulse, breath for breath:
    Speak low, lean low,
As long ago, my love, how long ago?

CHRISTINA ROSSETTI

326 · A FAREWELL

With all my will, but much against my heart,
We two now part.
My very dear,
Our solace is, the sad road lies so clear.
It needs no art,
With faint, averted feet
And many a tear,
In our opposed paths to persevere.
Go thou to east, I west.
We will not say
There's any hope, it is so far away.
But, O, my best,
When the one darling of our widowhead,
The nursling Grief,
Is dead,
And no dews blur our eyes
To see the peach-bloom come in evening skies,
Perchance we may,
Where now this night is day,
And even through faith of still averted feet,
Making full circle of our banishment,
Amazed meet;
The bitter journey to the bourne so sweet
Seasoning the termless feast of our content
With tears of recognition never dry.
                                    COVENTRY PATMORE

327 · LOVE'S MEMORIES

Love's memories haunt my footsteps still
    Like ceaseless flowings of the river.
Its mystic depths say what can fill?
    Sad disappointment waits forever.
                                    JOHN CLARE

When the lamp is shattered
The light in the dust lies dead;
When the cloud is scattered,
The rainbow's glory is shed.
When the lute is broken,
Sweet tones are remembered not;
When the lips have spoken,
Loved accents are soon forgot.

As music and splendor
Survive not the lamp and the lute,
The heart's echoes render
No song when the spirit is mute—
No song but sad dirges,
Like the wind through a ruined cell,
Or the mournful surges
That ring the dead seaman's knell.

When hearts have once mingled,
Love first leaves the well-built nest;
The weak one is singled
To endure what it once possessed.
O Love! who bewailest
The frailty of all things here,
Why choose you the frailest
For your cradle, your home, and your bier?

Its passions will rock thee
As the storms rock the ravens on high;
Bright reason will mock thee
Like the sun from a wintry sky.
From thy nest every rafter
Will rot, and thine eagle home
Leave thee naked to laughter,
When leaves fall and cold winds come.

PERCY BYSSHE SHELLEY

Maid of Athens, ere we part,
Give, oh give me back my heart!
Or, since that has left my breast,
Keep it now, and take the rest
Hear my vow before I go,
    Zoë mou, sas agapo.

By those tresses unconfined,
Woo'd by each Ægean wind;
By those lids whose jetty fringe
Kiss thy soft cheeks' blooming tinge;
By those wild eyes like the roe,
    Zoë mou, sas agapo.

By that lip I long to taste,
By that zone-encircled waist,
By all the token-flowers that tell
What words can never speak so well;
By love's alternate joy and woe,
    Zoë mou, sas agapo.

Maid of Athens! I am gone:
Think of me, sweet! when alone.
Though I fly to Istambol,
Athens holds my heart and soul:
Can I cease to love thee? No!
    Zoë mou, sas agapo.
        GEORGE GORDON, LORD BYRON

330 · SONNET

That thou hast her, it is not all my grief,
And yet it may be said I loved her dearly;
That she hath thee, is of my wailing chief,
A loss in love that touches me more nearly.
Loving offenders, thus I will excuse ye:
Thou dost love her, because thou know'st I love her;
And for my sake even so doth she abuse me,
Suffering my friend for my sake to approve her.
If I lose thee, my loss is my love's gain,
And losing her, my friend hath found that loss;
Both find each other, and I lose both twain,
And both for my sake lay on me this cross:
    But here's the joy; my friend and I are one;
    Sweet flattery! then she loves but me alone.

WILLIAM SHAKESPEARE

331 · SONNET

Farewell! thou art too dear for my possessing,
And like enough thou know'st thy estimate:
The charter of thy worth gives thee releasing;
My bonds in thee are all determinate.
For how do I hold thee but by thy granting?
And for that riches where is my deserving?
The cause of this fair gift in me is wanting,
And so my patent back again is swerving.
Thyself thou gavest, thy own worth then not knowing,
Or me, to whom thou gavest it, else mistaking;
So thy great gift, upon misprision growing,
Comes home again, on better judgement making.
    Thus have I had thee, as a dream doth flatter,
    In sleep a king, but waking no such matter.

WILLIAM SHAKESPEARE

332 · LOVE ME LITTLE, LOVE ME LONG

Love me little, love me long!
Is the burden of my song:
Love that is too hot and strong
    Burneth soon to waste.
Still I would not have thee cold—
Not too backward, nor too bold;
Love that lasteth till 'tis old
    Fadeth not in haste.
Love me little, love me long!
Is the burden of my song.

If thou lovest me too much,
'Twill not prove as true a touch;
Love me little more than such—
    For I fear the end.
I'm with little well content,
And a little from thee sent
Is enough, with true intent
    To be steadfast, friend.

Say thou lovest me, while thou live
I to thee my love will give,
Never dreaming to deceive
    While that life endures;
Nay, and after death, in sooth,
I to thee will keep my truth,
As now when in my May of youth:
    This my love assures.

Constant love is moderate ever,
And it will through life persever;
Give me that with true endeavor—
    I will it restore.

A suit of durance let it be,
For all weather—that for me—
For the land or for the sea:
 Lasting evermore.

Winter's cold or summer's heat,
Autumn's tempests on it beat;
It can never know defeat,
 Never can rebel:
Such the love that I would gain,
Such the love, I tell thee plain,
Thou must give, or woo in vain:
 So to thee—farewell!

AUTHOR UNKNOWN

333 · LOVE'S SECRET

Never seek to tell thy love,
 Love that never told can be;
For the gentle wind doth move
 Silently, invisibly.

I told my love, I told my love,
 I told her all my heart;
Trembling, cold, in ghastly fears,
 Ah! she did depart!

Soon after she was gone from me,
 A traveler came by,
Silently, invisibly:
 He took her with a sigh.

WILLIAM BLAKE

334 · REMEMBER

Remember me when I am gone away,
  Gone far away into the silent land;
  When you can no more hold me by the hand,
Nor I half turn to go, yet turning stay.
Remember me when no more day by day
  You tell me of our future that you planned:
  Only remember me; you understand
It will be late to counsel then or pray.
Yet if you should forget me for a while
  And afterwards remember, do not grieve:
  For if the darkness and corruption leave
  A vestige of thought that once I had,
Better by far you should forget and smile
  Than you should remember and be sad.

CHRISTINA ROSSETTI

335 · THE STOLEN HEART

I prythee send me back my heart
  Since I cannot have thine;
For if from yours you will not part,
  Why then shouldst thou have mine?

Yet now I think on't, let it lie;
  To find it were in vain,
For thou'st a thief in either eye
  Would steal it back again.

Why should two hearts in one breast lie,
  And yet not lodge together?
O love! where is thy sympathy,
  If thus our breasts you sever?

But love is such a mystery,
  I cannot find it out;
For when I think I'm best resolved,
  I then am most in doubt.

Then farewell love, and farewell woe,
  I will no longer pine;
For I'll believe I have her heart
  As much as she hath mine.

SIR JOHN SUCKLING

336 · A SILENT WOOD

O silent wood, I enter thee
With a heart so full of misery
For all the voices from the trees
And the ferns that cling about my knees.

In thy darkest shadow let me sit
When the gray owls about thee flit;
There will I ask of thee a boon,
That I may not faint or die or swoon.

Gazing through the gloom like one
Whose life and hopes are also done,
Frozen like a thing of stone
I sit in thy shadow—but not alone.

Can God bring back the day when we two stood
Beneath the clinging trees in that dark wood?

ELIZABETH SIDDAL

337 · A COMPLAINT

There is a change—and I am poor;
Your love hath been, nor long ago,
A fountain at my fond heart's door,
Whose only business was to flow;
And flow it did: not taking heed
Of its own bounty, or my need.

What happy moments did I count!
Blest was I then all bliss above!
Now, for that consecrated fount
Of murmuring, sparkling, living love,
What have I? shall I dare to tell?
A comfortless and hidden well.

A well of love—it may be deep—
I trust it is—and never dry:
What matter? if the waters sleep
In silence and obscurity.
—Such change, and at the very door
Of my fond heart, hath made me poor.
                    WILLIAM WORDSWORTH

338 · THOU HAST WOUNDED
THE SPIRIT THAT LOVED THEE

Thou hast wounded the spirit that loved thee,
    And cherished thine image for years,
Thou hast taught me at last to forget thee,
    In secret, in silence, and tears,
As a young bird when left by its mother,
    Its earliest pinions to try,
Round the nest will still lingering hover,
    Ere its trembling wings to try.

Thus we're taught in this cold world to smother
  Each feeling that once was so dear;
Like that young bird I'll seek to discover
  A home of affection elsewhere.
Though this heart may still cling to thee fondly
  And dream of sweet memories past,
Yet hope, like the rainbow of summer,
  Gives a promise of Lethe at last.

Like the sunbeams that play on the ocean,
  In tremulous touches of light,
Is the heart in its early emotion,
  Illumined with versions as bright.
Yet ofttimes beneath the waves swelling,
  A tempest will suddenly come,
All rudely and wildly dispelling
  The love of the happiest home.

MRS. DAVID PORTER

339 · HAD I A CAVE

Had I a cave on some wild, distant shore,
Where the winds howl to the waves' dashing roar,
    There would I weep my woes,
    There seek my lost repose,
    Till grief my eyes should close,
      Ne'er to wake more!

Falsest of womankind! canst thou declare
All thy fond-plighted vows—fleeting as air?
    To thy new lover hie,
    Laugh o'er thy perjury,
    Then in thy bosom try
      What peace is there!

ROBERT BURNS

When we two parted
  In silence and tears,
Half broken-hearted,
  To sever for years.
Pale grew thy cheek and cold,
  Colder thy kiss;
Truly that hour foretold
  Sorrow to this.

The dew of the morning
  Sunk chill on my brow—
It felt like the warning
  Of what I feel now.
Thy vows are all broken,
  And light is thy fame;
I hear thy name spoken,
  And share in its shame.

They name thee before me,
  A knell to mine ear;
A shudder comes o'er me—
  Why wert thou so dear?
They know not I knew thee,
  Who knew thee too well:
Long, long shall I rue thee,
  Too deeply to tell.

In secret we met—
  In silence I grieve,
That thy heart could forget,
  Thy spirit deceive.
If I should meet thee,
  After long years,
How should I greet thee?
  With silence and tears.

GEORGE GORDON, LORD BYRON

What should I say
Since faith is dead,
And truth alway
From you is fled?
Should I be led
With doubleness?
    Nay, nay, mistress!

I promised you
And you promised me
To be as true
As I would be;
But since I see
Your double heart,
    Farewell my part!

For though to take
It is not my mind
But to forsake—
I am not blind—
And as I find
So will I trust.
    Farewell, unjust!

Can ye say nay?
But you said
That I alway
Should be obeyed;
And thus betrayed
Or that I wist—
    Farewell, unkissed!
                    Sir Thomas Wyatt

342 · GROWN AND FLOWN

I loved my love from green of spring
   Until sere autumn's fall;
But now that leaves are withering
   How should one love at all?
   One heart's too small
For hunger, cold, love, everything.

I loved my love on sunny days
   Until late summer's wane;
But now that frost begins to glaze
   How should one love again?
   Nay, love and pain
Walk wide apart in diverse ways.

I loved my love—alas to see
   That this should be, alas!
I thought that this could scarcely be,
   Yet has it come to pass:
   Sweet sweet love was,
Now bitter bitter grown to me.
                   CHRISTINA ROSSETTI

343 · GO WHERE GLORY
WAITS THEE!

Go where glory waits thee;
But, while fame elates thee,
   O still remember me!
When the praise thou meetest
To thine ear is sweetest,
   O then remember me!
Other arms may press thee,

All the joys that bless thee
  Sweeter far may be;
But when friends are nearest,
And when joys are dearest,
  O then remember me!
When, at eve, thou rovest
By the star thou lovest,
  O then remember me!
Think when home returning,
Bright we've seen it burning,
  O thus remember me!
Oft as summer closes,
When thine eye reposes
On its lingering roses,
  Once so loved by thee,
Think of her who wove them,
Her who made thee love them;
  O then remember me!

When, around thee dying,
Autumn leaves are lying,
  O then remember me!
And, at night, when gazing
On the gay hearth blazing,
  O still remember me!
Then should music, stealing
All the soul of feeling,
To thy heart appealing,
  Draw one tear from thee—
Then let memory bring thee
Strains I used to sing thee;
  O then remember me!

THOMAS MOORE

Farewell has long been said; I have forgone thee;
   I never name thee even.
But how shall I learn virtues and yet shun thee?
   For thou art so near heaven
That heavenward meditations pause upon thee.

Thou dost beset the path to every shrine;
   My trembling thoughts discern
Thy goodness in the good for which I pine;
   And, if I turn from but one sin, I turn
Unto a smile of thine.

How shall I thrust thee apart
   Since all my growth tends to thee night and day—
To thee faith, hope, and art?
   Swift are the currents setting all one way;
They draw my life, my life, out of my heart.

ALICE MEYNELL

345 · SHE CAME AND WENT

As a twig trembles, which a bird
  Lights on to sing, then leaves unbent,
So is my memory thrilled and stirred—
  I only know she came and went.

As clasps some lake, by gusts unriven,
  The blue dome's measureless content,
So my soul held that moment's heaven—
  I only know she came and went.

As, at one bound, our swift spring heaps
  The orchards full of bloom and scent,
So clove her May my wintry sleeps—
  I only know she came and went.

An angel stood and met my gaze,
  Through the low doorway of my tent;
The tent is struck, the vision stays—
  I only know she came and went.

O, when the room grows slowly dim,
  And life's last oil is nearly spent,
One gush of light these eyes will brim,
  Only to think she came and went.

JAMES RUSSELL LOWELL

346 · SONNET

Youth gone, and beauty gone if ever there
   Dwelt beauty in so poor a face as this;
   Youth gone and beauty, what remains of bliss?
I will not bind fresh roses in my hair,
To shame a cheek at best but little fair—
   Leave youth his roses, who can bear a thorn—
I will not seek for blossoms anywhere,
   Except such common flowers as blow with corn.
Youth gone and beauty gone, what doth remain?
The longing of a heart pent up forlorn,
    A silent heart whose silence loves and longs;
    The silence of a heart which sang its songs
While youth and beauty made a summer morn,
Silence of love that cannot sing again.

CHRISTINA ROSSETTI

347 · DOWN BY THE SALLEY GARDENS

Down by the salley gardens my love and I
    did meet;
She passed the salley gardens with little snow-
    white feet.
She bid me take love easy, as the leaves grow
    on the tree;
But I, being young and foolish, with her
    would not agree.

In a field by the river my love and I did
    stand,
And on my leaning shoulder she laid her
    snow-white hand.

She bid me take life easy, as the grass grows
    on the weirs;
But I was young and foolish, and now am full
    of tears.

WILLIAM BUTLER YEATS

348 · EVEN SO

So it is, my dear.
All such things touch secret strings
    For heavy hearts to hear.
    So it is, my dear.

Very like indeed:
Sea and sky, afar, on high,
    Sand and strewn seaweed—
    Very like indeed.

But the sea stands spread
As one wall with the flat skies,
Where the lean black craft like flies
    Seem well-nigh stagnated,
    Soon to drop off dead.

Seemed it so to us
When I was thine and thou wast mine,
    And all these things were thus,
    But all our world in us?

Could we be so now?
Not if all beneath heaven's pall
    Lay dead but I and thou,
    Could we be so now!

DANTE GABRIEL ROSSETTI

349 · DEAD LOVE

Oh never weep for love that's dead
  Since love is seldom true
But changes his fashion from blue to red,
  From brightest red to blue,
And love was born to an early death
  And is so seldom true.

Then harbor no smile on your bonny face
  To win the deepest sigh.
The fairest words on truest lips
  Pass on and surely die,
And you will stand alone, my dear,
  When wintry winds draw nigh.

Sweet, never weep for what cannot be,
  For this God has not given.
If the merest dream of love were true
  Then, sweet, we should be in heaven,
And this is only earth, my dear,
  Where true love is not given.

ELIZABETH SIDDAL

350 · AN END

Love, strong as Death, is dead.
Come, let us make his bed
Among the dying flowers:
A green turf at his head;
And a stone at his feet,
Whereon we may sit
In the quiet evening hours.

He was born in the spring,
And died before the harvesting:
On the last warm summer day
He left us; he would not stay
For autumn twilight cold and gray.
Sit we by his grave, and sing
He is gone away.

To few chords and sad and low
Sing we so:
Be our eyes fixed on the grass
Shadow-veiled as the years pass,
While we think of all that was
In the long ago.

CHRISTINA ROSSETTI

351 · ECHOES AND MEMORIES

Music, when soft voices die,
Vibrates in the memory—
Odors, when sweet violets sicken,
Live within the sense they quicken.

Rose leaves, when the rose is dead,
Are heaped for the belovèd's bed;
And so thy thoughts, when thou art gone,
Love itself shall slumber on.

PERCY BYSSHE SHELLEY

352 · THE GARDEN OF LOVE

I went to the Garden of Love,
And saw what I never had seen:
A chapel was built in the midst,
Where I used to play on the green.

And the gates of this chapel were shut,
And "Thou shalt not" writ over the door;
So I turn'd to the Garden of Love
That so many sweet flowers bore;

And I saw it was filled with graves,
And tombstones where flowers should be;
And priests in black gowns were walking their rounds,
And binding with briars my joys and desires.

WILLIAM BLAKE

353 · ANNABEL LEE

It was many and many a year ago,
   In a kingdom by the sea,
That a maiden there lived whom you may know
   By the name of Annabel Lee;
And this maiden she lived with no other thought
   Than to love and be loved by me.

I was a child and she was a child,
   In this kingdom by the sea,
But we loved with a love that was more than love,
   I and my Annabel Lee;
With a love that the wingèd seraphs of heaven
   Coveted her and me.

And this was the reason that, long ago,
  In this kingdom by the sea,
A wind blew out of a cloud, chilling
  My beautiful Annabel Lee;
So that her highborn kinsman came
  And bore her away from me,
To shut her up in a sepulcher
  In this kingdom by the sea.

The angels, not half so happy in heaven,
  Went envying her and me;
Yes! that was the reason (as all men know,
  In this kingdom by the sea)
That the wind came out of the cloud by night,
  Chilling and killing my Annabel Lee.

But our love it was stronger by far than the love
  Of those who were older than we,
  Of many far wiser than we;
And neither the angels in heaven above,
  Nor the demons down under the sea,
Can ever dissever my soul from the soul
  Of the beautiful Annabel Lee:

For the moon never beams, without bringing me
      dreams
  Of the beautiful Annabel Lee;
And the stars never rise, but I feel the bright eyes
  Of the beautiful Annabel Lee;
And so, all the night-tide, I lie down by the side
Of my darling—my darling—my life and my bride,
  In her sepulcher there by the sea,
  In her tomb by the sounding sea.

EDGAR ALLAN POE

Thou wast all that to me, love,
  For which my soul did pine:
A green isle in the sea, love,
  A fountain and a shrine
All wreathed with fairy fruits and flowers,
  And all the flowers were mine.

Ah, dream too bright to last!
  Ah, starry hope, that didst arise
But to be overcast!
  A voice from out the future cries,
"On! on!"—but o'er the past
  (Dim gulf) my spirit hovering lies
Mute, motionless, aghast.

For, alas! alas! with me
  The light of life is o'er!
No more—no more—no more—
(Such language holds the solemn sea
  To the sands upon the shore!)
Shall bloom the thunder-blasted tree,
  Or the stricken eagle soar.

And all my days are trances,
  And all my nightly dreams
Are where thy gray eye glances,
  And where thy footstep gleams—
In what ethereal dances,
  By what eternal streams.

                            EDGAR ALLAN POE

355 · HOW RICH THAT FOREHEAD'S
CALM EXPANSE!

How rich that forehead's calm expanse!
How bright that heaven-directed glance!
—Waft her to glory, wingèd powers,
Ere sorrow be renewed,
And intercourse with mortal hours
Bring back a humbler mood!
So looked Cecilia when she drew
An angel from his station;
So looked; not ceasing to pursue
Her tuneful adoration!
But hand and voice alike are still;
No sound *here* sweeps away the will
That gave it birth: in service meek
One upright arm sustains the cheek,
And one across the bosom lies—
That rose, and now forgets to rise,
Subdued by breathless harmonies
Of meditative feeling;
Mute strains from worlds beyond the skies,
Through the pure light of female eyes,
Their sanctity revealing!

WILLIAM WORDSWORTH

356 · SONNET

Belovèd, my belovèd, when I think
That thou wast in the world a year ago,
What time I sat alone here in the snow
And saw no footprint, heard the silence sink
No moment at thy voice . . . but, link by link,
Went counting all my chains as if that so
They never could fall off at any blow
Struck by thy possible hand . . . why, thus I drink
Of life's great cup of wonder! Wonderful,
Never to feel thee thrill the day or night
With personal act or speech—nor even cull
Some prescience of thee with the blossoms white
Thou sawest growing! Atheists are as dull,
Who cannot guess God's presence out of sight.

ELIZABETH BARRETT BROWNING

357 · OH! SNATCH'D AWAY
IN BEAUTY'S BLOOM

Oh! snatch'd away in beauty's bloom,
On thee shall press no ponderous tomb;
    But on thy turf shall roses rear
    Their leaves, the earliest of the year;
And the wild cypress wave in tender gloom:

And oft by yon blue gushing stream
    Shall Sorrow lean her drooping head,
And feed deep thought with many a dream,
    and lingering pause and lightly tread;
    Fond wretch! as if her step disturb'd the dead!

Away! we know that tears are vain,
    That death nor heeds nor hears distress;
Will this unteach us to complain?
    Or make one mourner weep the less?
And thou—who tell'st me to forget,
Thy looks are wan, thine eyes are wet.

GEORGE GORDON, LORD BYRON

358 · SHE DWELT AMONG
THE UNTRODDEN WAYS

She dwelt among the untrodden ways
    Beside the springs of dove,
A maid whom there were none to praise
    And very few to love:

A violet by a mossy stone
    Half hidden from the eye!
—Fair as a star, when only one
    Is shining in the sky.

She lived unknown, and few could know
    When Lucy ceased to be;
But she is in her grave, and, oh,
    The difference to me!

WILLIAM WORDSWORTH

359 · LOVE'S GUERDONS

Dearest, if I almost cease to weep for you,
  Do not doubt I love you just the same;
'Tis because my life has grown to keep for you
  All the hours that sorrow does not claim.

All the hours when I may steal away to you,
  Where you lie alone through the long day,
Lean my face against your turf and say to you
  All that there is no one else to say.

Do they let you listen—do you lean to me?
  Know now what in life you never knew,
When I whisper all that you have been to me,
  All that I might never be to you?

Dear, lie still. No tears but mine are shed for you,
  No one else leaves kisses day by day,
No one's heart but mine has beat and bled for you,
  No one else's flowers push mine away.

No one else remembers—do not call to her,
  Not alone she treads the churchyard grass;
You are nothing now who once were all to her,
  Do not call her—let the strangers pass!

E. Nesbit

I sleep with thee, and wake with thee,
  And yet thou art not there;
I fill my arms with thoughts of thee,
  And press the common air.
Thy eyes are gazing upon mine,
  When thou art out of sight;
My lips are always touching thine,
  At morning, noon, and night.

I think and speak of other things
  To keep my mind at rest:
But still to thee my memory clings
  Like love in woman's breast.
I hide it from the world's wide eye,
  And think and speak contrary;
But soft the wind comes from the sky,
  And whispers tales of Mary.

The night wind whispers in my ear,
  The moon shines in my face;
A burden still of chilling fear
  I find in every place.
The breeze is whispering in the bush,
  And the dews fall from the tree,
All sighing on, and will not hush,
  Some pleasant tales of thee.
                                    JOHN CLARE

When stars are in the quiet skies,
  Then most I pine for thee;
Bend on me, then, thy tender eyes,
  As stars look on the sea!

For thoughts, like waves that glide by night,
  Are stillest when they shine;
Mine earthly love lies hushed in light
  Beneath the heaven of thine.

There is an hour when angels keep
  Familiar watch o'er men,
When coarser souls are wrapped in sleep—
  Sweet spirit, meet me then.

There is an hour when holy dreams
  Through slumber fairest glide;
And in that mystic hour it seems
  Thou shouldst be by my side.

My thoughts of thee too sacred are
  For daylight's common beam:
I can but know thee as my star,
  My angel and my dream!

EDWARD BULWER-LYTTON

When I am dead, my dearest,
Sing no sad songs for me;
Plant thou no roses at my head,
Nor shady cypress tree:
Be the green grass above me
With showers and dewdrops wet;
And if thou wilt, remember,
And if thou wilt, forget.

I shall not see the shadows,
I shall not feel the rain;
I shall not hear the nightingale
Sing on, as if in pain;
And dreaming through the twilight
That doth not rise nor set,
Haply I may remember,
And haply may forget.

CHRISTINA ROSSETTI

No more summer for Molly and me;
    There is snow on the tree,
And the blackbirds plump large as the rooks are, almost,
    And the water is hard
Where they used to dip bills at the dawn ere her figure
        was lost
    To these coasts, now my prison close-barred.

No more planting by Molly and me
    Where the beds used to be
Of sweet-william; no training the clambering rose
    By the framework of fir
Now bowering the pathway, whereon it swings gaily
        and blows
    As if calling commendment from her.

No more jauntings by Molly and me
    To the town by the sea,
Or along over Whitesheet to Wynyard's green Gap,
    Catching Montacute Crest
To the right against Sedgmoor, and Corton-Hill's far-
        distant cap,
    And Pilsdon and Lewsdon to west.

No more singing by Molly to me
    In the evenings when she
Was in mood and in voice, and the candles were lit,
    And past the porch-quoin
The rays would spring out on the laurels; and dumble-
        dores hit
    On the pane, as if wishing to join.

Where, then, is Molly, who's no more with me?
    —As I stand on this lea,
Thinking thus, there's a many-flamed star in the air,

That tosses a sign
That her glance is regarding its face from her home, so
    that there
Her eyes may have meetings with mine.

Thomas Hardy

364 · SURPRISED BY JOY

Surprised by joy—impatient as the wind
I turned to share the transport—Oh! with whom
But thee, deep buried in the silent tomb,
That spot which no vicissitude can find?
Love, faithful love, recalled thee to my mind—
But how could I forget thee? Through what power,
Even for the least division of an hour,
Have I been so beguiled as to be blind
To my most grievous loss!—That thought's return
Was the worst pang that sorrow ever bore,
Save one, one only, when I stood forlorn,
Knowing my heart's best treasure was no more;
That neither present time, nor years unborn
Could to my sight that heavenly face restore.

William Wordsworth

365 · A REMEMBRANCE

I see thee still! Thou art not dead,
  Though dust is mingled with thy form;
The broken sunbeam hath not shed
  The final rainbow on the storm:
In visions of the midnight deep,
  Thine accents through my bosom thrill
Till joy's fond impulse bids me weep—
  For, wrapt in thought, I see thee still!

I see thee still—that cheek of rose—
  Those lips with dewy fragrance wet—
That forehead in serene repose—
  Those soul-lit eyes—I see them yet!
Sweet seraph! Sure thou art not dead,
  Thou gracest still this earthly sphere;
An influence still is round me shed,
  Like thine—and yet thou art not here!

Farewell, beloved! To mortal sight
  Thy vermeil cheek no more may bloom;
No more thy smiles inspire delight,
  For thou art garnered in the tomb—
Rich harvest for that ruthless power
  Which hath me bound to bear his will:
Yet, as in hope's unclouded hour,
  Throned in my heart I see thee still.

WILLIS GAYLORD CLARKE

INDEX OF POETS